PLATE I

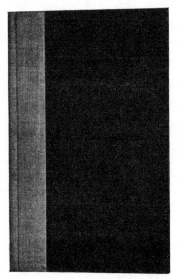

Quarter-bound—Cloth back and paper sides

Half-bound—Cloth back and corners and paper sides

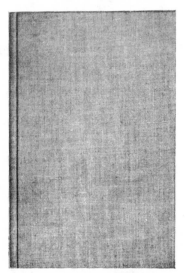

Full-bound—complete cloth cover

Half-bound—Alternative—cloth back and edges and paper sides

STYLES OF BINDING

# BASIC BOOK-BINDING

BY A. W. LEWIS

DOVER PUBLICATIONS, INC.,
NEW YORK

To
HELEN
a "craft widow" for
many years

*International Standard Book Number: 0-486-20169-4*
*Library of Congress Catalog Card Number: 57-13426*

Manufactured in the United States of America
Dover Publications, Inc.
180 Varick Street
New York, N. Y. 10014

# PREFACE

ALTHOUGH a number of books already exist which deal reasonably fully with bookcrafts and also with advanced bookbinding, few of them cover in any detail the basic methods of binding in the simpler styles. This book is an attempt to bridge the gap by supplying step by step instructions in the essential operations involved in the binding of books by hand in cloth and in library style.

No preliminary "bookcrafts" is suggested as it is believed that sufficient preparatory work can be done in bookbinding itself by the making up of small books of plain writing or drawing paper before starting on books of any value.

Deliberate omission has been made of any reference to cover decoration since it is felt that the addition of patterns to the covers of utilitarian books of this kind is inappropriate —reliance should be made entirely on the careful choice of colour and texture in the materials used.

It is hoped that this book will be found useful in training colleges, art schools, secondary schools and in evening classes and also that sufficient detailed instruction is given to enable a student, working on his own, to do so with success.

Thanks are expressed to numerous students at the Loughborough College Summer School classes in bookbinding who so readily helped by their criticism of the original manuscript, and also to Mr. A. F. Bond who produced the photographs.

*Summer*, 1952                                                    A.W.L.

# CONTENTS

*Page*

PREFACE       vii

LIST OF PLATES       xi

*Chapter*

I   EQUIPMENT — Folder—knife—brushes—scissors—saw—hammer—safety cutting edge—try square—spring dividers—knocking-down iron—oilstone—glue-kettle — needles — awl — paring knife — strop — paring stone—sewing frame—card cutter—nipping press—standing press—lying press and plough—cutting boards —backing boards—pressing boards—hand-tool letters —pallet—small patterned tools—finishing stove       1

II   MATERIALS — Paper — boards — cloth — leather — sheepskins—miscellaneous materials—adhesives       9

III   BASIC OPERATIONS—Folding—cutting—cutting a pair of boards—cutting a pair of boards with a card cutter—sharpening a knife—sharpening a plough blade —pasting—tipping—turning-in an overlap—handling a large pasted sheet—rubbing down—pressing—nipping —preparation of paste—preparation of glue       19

IV   BINDING A SINGLE-SECTIONED BOOK — Preparing the endpapers—marking up for sewing—sewing a single-sectioned book—marking out for cutting the fore-edge—cutting the edges with the plough—marking out for cutting head and ail—preparing the boards—attaching the boards to the book—cutting patterns for the cloth back and corners—covering the back—preparing the sides—pasting down the endpapers—alternative endpaper for single sectioned books—alternative styles of binding for a single-sectioned book       33

V   PREPARING A MULTI-SECTIONED BOOK FOR REBINDING — Pulling — signatures — pulling tight-backed books — knocking out the groove — pressing the sections—cutting guards—mending torn sections—guarding single sheets and plates—collating       47

*Chapter* *Page*

VI CASE-BOUND BOOKS—Cased book, rounded and backed—knocking-up square at the head and the back—marking-up for sewing on tapes—setting up the sewing frame—sewing the sections on tapes—making a kettle-stitch—joining thread—finishing off the sewing—knocking down the swelling—pasting-up first and last sections—tipping-on the endpapers—gluing-up the back—cutting the fore-edge—rounding the back—backing the book—lining-up the back with mull—lining-up the back with paper—cutting the boards to size—cutting the head—cutting the tail—sticking down the tapes and mull—making a case—casing the book—flat-back book—round-back book  54

VII ENDPAPERS—Zig-zag endpapers—"made" endpapers—cloth jointed endpapers  81

VIII HOLLOW-BACKED BINDING—Sewing on the endpapers—pasting-up the endpapers—attaching the boards to the book—attaching the hollow back—slitting—covering the hollow-backed book—siding a quarter-bound book—pasting-down endpapers  88

IX LIBRARY STYLE BINDING — Making split-boards—allowance for the French groove—preparing the slips—attaching the split-boards—preparing the leather for the back and corners—paring the leather—paring the corners—pasting the leather—attaching the leather corners—attaching the leather back—setting the headcaps—trimming the leather—siding—trimming-out inside—pasting-down shut  96

X BINDING SINGLE SHEETS—Gluing-up the back—cutting the boards to size—preparing the hinged boards—attaching the boards to the book—stab-sewing the book—covering the back with cloth—marking and cutting the edges—siding the book—lining the boards—alternative method of binding single sheets—over-sewing or whip-stitching  112

XI LETTERING A BOOK — Written labels—tooled labels using the hand tools—lettering with printer's ink—lettering with the heated tools and carbon paper—heating the tools for lettering—lettering with gold film or gold foil—tooling on the spine—tooling on the side—blind tooling on leather—tooling the spines of library style books  120

APPENDIX  131

SUPPLIERS OF MATERIALS  137

INDEX  139

# LIST OF PLATES

*Plate*

I   Styles of Binding       *Frontispiece*

II   Bookbinding Equipment—1       *Page* 2

III   Bookbinding Equipment—2       ,,  4

IV   Bookbinding Equipment—3       ,,  6

V   Bookbinding Equipment—4       ,,  8

VI   Cutting with Straight-edge and Knife—Rubbing-down through Paper—Attaching the Board       *Facing Page* 36

VII   Handling a Large Pasted Sheet       ,,  ,,  37

VIII   Collating       ,,  ,,  52

IX   Knocking-up Square at Head and Back       ,,  ,,  53

X   Paring Leather with an Edging Knife — Ensuring that the Leather Adheres to the Spine       ,,  ,,  120

XI   Method of Using Hand Tools—Retouching a Faulty Impression—Tooling the Spine       ,,  ,,  121

## NOTES ON TERMS AND PRACTICES

Bookbinding and bookbinding terminology are largely uniform in the English-speaking world. There are, however, minor variations, not only between the United States and Great Britain, but also between different parts of the United States. The following terms require some comment.

**CARTRIDGE PAPER.** This term is not generally used in the United States. American binders use a paper which is called simply "endpaper," or "end leaves," or "linings." This ranges in weight from 60 to 80 pound stock; 70 pound is most commonly used.

**LINSON.** This term is not used in the United States, although many corresponding products are available, usually under manufacturers' trade names. "Linnette" is one such imitation cloth. "Leatherette" is a similar product which in surface finish imitates leather.

**ART PAPER.** This is called "coated stock" or "slick paper" in the United States. While it is used extensively in printing, it is not suitable for bookbinding.

**STRAWBOARD.** Strawboard is not generally obtainable in the United States. Binders use, instead, pasteboard or binders board.

**ENGLISH FIBREBOARD.** This is called "pasteboard" in the United States. It is sold in point sizes: 70-75 point, 80-85 point, and 90-95 point. It is suitable for small or average-sized books, but has a tendency to warp if too thin a sheet is used on a large book. American binders, it must be observed, on the whole prefer a thicker board than do British binders.

**MILLBOARD.** This is usually called binders board in America. It is the best board in general use, and may be purchased in four weights: 70, 80, 88, and 98 point.

**OILED BOARDS.** Not generally used in the United States.

**TAPE.** Tape bindings are much less frequent in the United States. Most American commercial bindings are sewn in signatures without tape, rounded and backed, fitted with muslin, and then placed in boards.

**BACKING AND ROUNDING.** National tastes vary considerably in the degree of rounding and the size of the sleeve. American binders on the whole prefer a shallower back and a looser board fit than do British binders.

# Chapter I

# EQUIPMENT

THE following list of equipment suggests the basic items necessary to start bookbinding. Improvisation is possible in some cases but inevitably it can only be second best and the traditional tools are to be preferred.

**FOLDER.** A bone folder about 6″ long is convenient for general work. Some folders made of plastic material wear away very quickly and often leave white marks when rubbed on cloth and should therefore be avoided.

**KNIFE.** A good sharp penknife is the best for general use with possibly a stouter cardboard knife for heavier work.

**BRUSHES.** Large brushes, not less than 1″ across should be used, they are much more efficient than small ones as they enable pasting and gluing to be done quickly and evenly.

**SCISSORS.** A pair of scissors, large ones for preference, are needed for odd trimming jobs.

**SAW.** A small tenon saw for sawing-in the kettle-stitch marks before sewing.

**HAMMER.** Any hammer will serve if used with care but the bookbinder's hammer, similar to a shoemaker's hammer, with a large rounded face and with a cross pane is best.

**SAFETY CUTTING EDGE.** One of polished wood with a metal edge is the best type. Avoid the bent, all-metal pattern as it easily gets dented and as a result becomes useless for cutting clean, straight edges.

**TRY SQUARE.** An ordinary 6″ square as used by the carpenter.

1

*PLATE II*

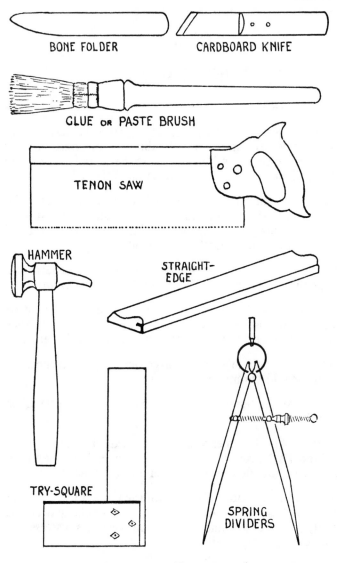

BONE FOLDER    CARDBOARD KNIFE

GLUE or PASTE BRUSH

TENON SAW

HAMMER

STRAIGHT-EDGE

TRY-SQUARE

SPRING DIVIDERS

BOOKBINDING EQUIPMENT—1

**SPRING DIVIDERS.** Dividers of any kind may be used but the spring pattern are the most useful.

**KNOCKING-DOWN IRON.** A suitable size is about 8″ by $3\frac{1}{2}$″. An ordinary old-type flat iron makes an excellent substitute.

**OILSTONE.** An oilstone is essential for the maintenance of sharp edges on cutting tools. A medium or fine India or Washita stone 8″ by 2″, with a can of good lubricating oil.

**GLUE KETTLE.** A glue-pot with a water-bath is required. The water-bath is essential to avoid burning the glue.

**NEEDLES.** Bookbinder's needles, or any stout needle with the eye large enough to take the thread comfortably.

**AWL.** A fine awl for making holes for the needle is useful on occasion.

**PARING KNIFE.** Paring knives of various patterns are used according to the taste of the worker. The wide French knife, the ordinary cobbler's knife or the edging knife.

**STROP.** A strop can be made from a piece of wood about 2″ wide and 12″ long. A strip of leather, flesh side uppermost, is glued to one side and a strip of fine emery cloth to the other. The leather is coated with fine emery paste— motorist's fine valve-grinding paste does excellently.

**PARING STONE.** A lithographer's stone is the most suitable but any heavy stone with a smooth surface or a sheet of plate-glass will serve as a substitute on which to pare the leather.

**SEWING FRAME.** A simple frame consisting of a board about 12″ long by 9″ wide with two uprights and a cross-bar 3″ to 4″ above the board is all that is required for most books sewn on tapes.

*PLATE III*

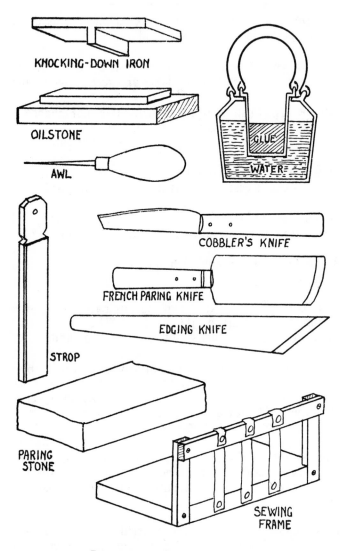

KNOCKING-DOWN IRON

OILSTONE

AWL

GLUE

WATER

STROP

COBBLER'S KNIFE

FRENCH PARING KNIFE

EDGING KNIFE

PARING STONE

SEWING FRAME

BOOKBINDING EQUIPMENT—2

CARD CUTTER. A card cutter with a blade about 15″ long simplifies the work of preparing boards very considerably but card cutting can be done with a knife and straight-edge or by means of the plough and press.

NIPPING PRESS. A nipping press for quick and even pressing is very necessary. Old iron letter presses can usually be bought quite cheaply and are very efficient. The sizes are about 12″ by 10″ and 18″ by 12″.

STANDING PRESS. A standing press is not required to give as much pressure as the nipping press and is used for holding the books flat while they are drying out. Various forms exist but a press can be improvised in emergency by means of a weight on top of two pressing boards.

LYING PRESS AND PLOUGH. This is essential as it is the bookbinder's main piece of apparatus. A fair sized heavy press is recommended. A plough with an adjustable blade is best since it enables the blade to be removed easily for the sharpening operation which so frequently recurs. A "tub" or stand for the press is also needed and it should be about 30″ high.

CUTTING BOARDS. Wedge-shaped boards of beech with the top edges square. Three pairs are useful, say, 8″, 12″ and 15″ long.

BACKING BOARDS. Wedge-shaped boards of beech with the top edges sloped off at an angle of about 80 degrees. Three pairs, 8″, 10″, and 15″ long.

PRESSING BOARDS. Used with the nipping and standing presses. Boards made of multi-ply wood are most useful. Pairs to fit the size of the press and a few smaller ones, e.g., 12″ by 10″; 11″ by 7″; 10″ by 6″; and 8″ by 5″, will be found useful.

HAND-TOOL LETTERS. All "finishing" tools, i.e., tools for

*PLATE IV*

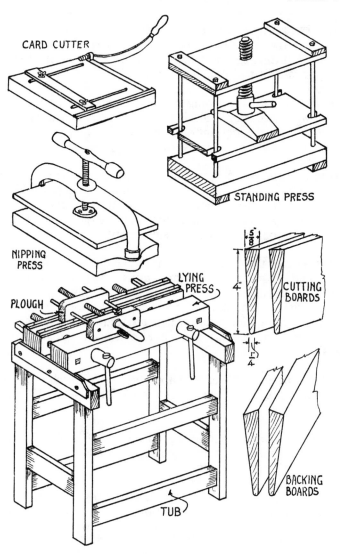

CARD CUTTER

STANDING PRESS

NIPPING PRESS

PLOUGH

LYING PRESS

CUTTING BOARDS

BACKING BOARDS

TUB

BOOKBINDING EQUIPMENT—3

lettering and decoration are made of brass and are fitted with wooden handles. Various sizes of letter are available. A set in which the letters are $\frac{3}{16}''$ high is a good size to start with and sets of $\frac{1}{8}''$ and $\frac{1}{4}''$ letters can be added as required. These three sets will be found adequate for most needs. The sets should all be of the same style of letter so that they can be used together if required.

**PALLET.** Pallets are tools for impressing straight lines. They vary in length from $\frac{1}{4}''$ up to $4''$, but one which is about $2''$ to $2\frac{1}{2}''$ long will be most generally useful.

**SMALL PATTERNED TOOLS.** There is an infinite variety of these tools available but only one very simple tool is required at first. Choose a simple pattern such as the one illustrated and add others as the need arises. Simple tools can quite easily be made by filing the end of a $3''$ piece of brass rod and then polishing the surface on "flour" emery-cloth.

**FINISHING STOVE.** Some form of finishing stove for heating the tools will be required—the gas finishing stove, illustrated, is very satisfactory, electric ones are also obtainable. The common gas-ring could be adapted for the purpose.

*PLATE V*

## PRESSING BOARDS

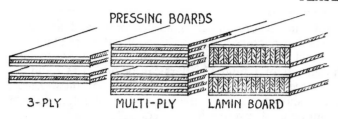

3-PLY      MULTI-PLY      LAMIN BOARD

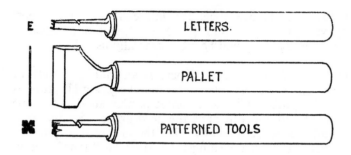

E    LETTERS.

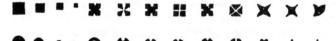

PALLET

PATTERNED TOOLS

SIMPLE PATTERNS EASILY FILED FROM BRASS ROD

BLANKS OF ROUND AND
SQUARE BRASS RODS.
HANDLES CAN BE $5\frac{1}{2}''$ OF
WOOD DOWEL ROD $\frac{5}{8}''$ TO $\frac{3}{4}''$ DIA.

$1\frac{1}{4}''$

$3''$

GAS FINISHING STOVE

BOOKBINDING EQUIPMENT—4

# Chapter II

# MATERIALS

GREAT care should be taken over the selection of suitable materials for bookbinding as satisfactory work can only be produced when the materials used are of good quality; an added advantage is that, besides giving a first-class product, materials of good quality are also much easier to work. All imitations should be avoided as they are merely a form of deception; the frank use of a material in its natural state, making the most of its own particular qualities, is much to be preferred. There is nothing to be gained by the use of papers which imitate cloth, cloth which is grained to look like leather or cheap leather stamped with the grain of more expensive kinds. Each material has a distinctive quality of its own which is destroyed as soon as it is made to ape the qualities of a different substance.

## PAPER

Paper is usually sold by the ream of 480 sheets or by the quire of 24 sheets—20 quires making one ream. The sheets are of various standard sizes the more usual of which are listed overleaf.

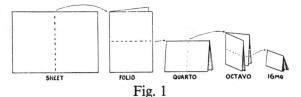

Fig. 1

The various sub-divisions indicated above are obtained by folding the standard size of sheet—unless otherwise stated it is always the longest side of the sheet which is folded in two (fig. 1).

| Name | Sheet | Folio (Fol.) | Quarto (4to.) | Octavo (8vo.) | Sexto-decimo (16mo.) |
|---|---|---|---|---|---|
| Imperial .. | 30 × 22 | 22 × 15 | 15× 11 | 11 × 7½ | 7½×5½ |
| Double-Crown.. | 30 ×20 | 20 ×15 | 15 ×10 | 10 ×7½ | 7½×5 |
| Royal .. .. | 25 ×20 | 20 ×12½ | 12½×10 | 10 ×6¼ | 6¼×5 |
| Medium .. | 24 ×19 | 19 ×12 | 12 × 9½ | 9½×6 | 6 ×4¾ |
| Demy .. .. | 22½×17½ | 17½×11¼ | 11¼× 8¾ | 8¾×5⅝ | 5⅝×4⅜ |
| Crown .. .. | 20 ×15 | 15 ×10 | 10 × 7½ | 7½×5 | 5 ×3¾ |
| Foolscap .. | 17 ×13½ | 13½× 8½ | 8½× 6¾ | 6¾×4¼ | 4¼×3⅜ |

The above sizes are given in inches.

*Folio* (*Fol.*)—is formed by folding the standard sheet once so that two leaves are produced.

*Quarto* (4*to*)—a second fold across the folio produces four leaves.

*Octavo* (8*vo*)—Quarto folded again gives eight leaves.

*Sexto-decimo* (16*mo*)—Octavo folded gives sixteen leaves.

Note that the terms folio, quarto, octavo, etc., refer only to the number of times a sheet has been folded and *not* to its size; the size is determined by the size of the original sheet and this is always placed first when size is indicated, e.g., Crown Quarto (Cr. 4to) measures 10″ by 7½″, while Royal Quarto (Roy. 4to) is 12½″ by 10″.

The weight of a ream of paper gives an indication of the thickness of the sheets, e.g., the weight of a ream of Imperial size paper could vary from about 72 lb., for thick paper as used in account books, down to about 30 lb. for a ream of thin cartridge paper.

Some common uses for the various sizes of paper are shown below.

Foolscap .. School exercise books—usually quarto, 8½″ by 6¾″.

Crown .. Novels—usually octavo, 7½″ by 5″.

Demy        ..   Text books—usually octavo, $8\frac{3}{4}''$ by $5\frac{5}{8}''$.
Medium      ..   Large books—usually octavo, $9\frac{1}{2}''$ by $6''$.
Royal       ..   Catalogues—usually octavo, $10''$ by $6\frac{1}{4}''$.
Imperial    ..   Portfolios, etc.

The size of this book is Crown octavo and the weight of the paper is 47 lb. per ream of $25''$ by $38''$ size sheets.

CARTRIDGE PAPER. A medium weight cartridge paper is very suitable for the making of endpapers. Paper weighing from 40 lb. to 50 lb. per ream is about the right thickness. As far as possible the cartridge paper should be chosen to match the tone of the paper in the book. Cartridge paper is usually sold in the Imperial size, $30''$ by $22''$.

HAND MADE PAPER. If the paper of the book is hand made then the endpapers must also be of the same material. It should be used for all best quality work.

COLOURED PAPER. A wide variety of coloured papers suitable for endpapers and for covering the sides of books is available from most suppliers. A good quality pastel paper is very suitable for this purpose. The usual size is Double-Crown, $30''$ by $20''$.

LINSON. This material, called Linson fabric by the manufacturers, is in fact a tough fibrous paper, often mistaken for cloth when the surface is embossed to imitate linen. It is an excellent covering material, it will stand up to hard pasting and has the additional advantage that the surface can be gently rubbed with a damp sponge to remove paste and finger marks. Linson is available in numerous colours and surface finishes. The cover of this book is of Linson.

PATTERNED PAPERS. An infinite assortment of printed patterned papers is on the market for use both as endpapers and as cover papers. They should be selected and used with discretion or they will not improve the appearance of the book. Large patterns should be avoided as they are not suited to the small areas of book surfaces. The usual size of patterned papers is Royal, 25″ by 20″.

MARBLED PAPERS. Good quality marbled paper wears well as sides on half-bound books and it can also be used for endpapers, in either case the pattern should be suited to the nature of the book. The usual size of marbled papers is Royal, 25″ by 20″.

BANK PAPER. This is thin, strong paper similar to that used for typewriting and is used for guards and for repairing the back of damaged sections.

JAPANESE VELLUM. Is similar to bank paper and is very strong and is used for the best work as guards and mending strips.

MANILLA. This is very thick paper—almost thin cardboard—and is useful for filling-in and for small, split boards. Available in Double-Crown size, 30″ by 20″.

ART PAPER. This is very glossy paper having its surface heavily dressed with china clay and should be avoided as it is quite unsuitable for any good quality bookbinding work.

KITCHEN PAPER. Is very useful as a cheap, white waste paper for use in pressing, etc. It can be bought in rolls or cut sheets.

NEWSPAPERS. An endless supply of old newspapers will be necessary to act as waste for pasting upon.

## BOARDS

STRAWBOARD. Strawboard is of a yellow colour and, as its name implies, is made from straw; it was mainly imported from Holland and is commonly referred to as Dutch strawboard. It is rather brittle and easily cracks on bending sharply and should be used for nothing better than case-bound books. It is quite suitable as the inside lining for a split-board provided that a tougher board is used on the outside.

The standard size of strawboard is 32″ by 22″ and it is the weight of *one* such board that is used as the standard for grading the thickness. The most useful sizes are 8 oz., 12 oz., 1 lb., 1½ lb. and 2 lb. boards, other thicknesses, when required, being obtained by gluing together thinner boards. Glued sheets will, in fact, make a board which is stiffer than a single sheet of the same thickness.

Strawboard is sold by weight, usually in half-hundred-weight bundles.

| Weight of One Strawboard Sheet | 8 oz. | 12 oz. | 1 lb. | 1½ lb. | 2 lb. |
|---|---|---|---|---|---|
| Approximate thickness of boards in inches .. | $\frac{1}{32}$ | $\frac{3}{64}$ | $\frac{1}{16}$ | $\frac{1}{12}$ | $\frac{1}{10}$ |
| Approximate number of boards in ½-cwt. bundle | 112 | 75 | 56 | 37 | 28 |

**ENGLISH FIBRE-BOARD.** This is grey in colour and tougher and slightly more expensive than strawboard. It is quite satisfactory for most books sewn on tapes. Its thickness is usually stated in decimals of an inch and the ·06 boards are approximately the same thickness as 1 lb. strawboard.

**MILLBOARD.** The best quality millboard is nearly black in colour and is very strong and tough. It is made from the fibres of old tarred ropes. Millboard is essential for all books which have the cords laced into the boards and it should always be used for the best work on tapes. It is the most efficient board for bookbinding and, as would be expected, the most expensive.

Millboard is sold by weight but is usually obtainable by the sheet in six standard thicknesses which are indicated by the cost of the sheet in the distant past.

| Name | Abbreviation | Approximate thickness |
|---|---|---|
| Sixpenny .. .. .. | 6 p | $\frac{1}{32}$ inch |
| Sevenpenny .. .. .. | 7p | $\frac{1}{16}$ inch |
| Eightpenny ... .. .. | 8p | $\frac{5}{64}$ inch |
| Eightpenny one cross .. .. | 8px | $\frac{7}{64}$ inch |
| Eightpenny two cross .. .. | 8pxx | $\frac{1}{8}$ inch |
| Tenpenny.. .. .. .. | 10p | $\frac{9}{64}$ inch |

Millboard sizes are slightly larger than the corresponding paper sizes and are listed below.

| Name | Abbreviation | Size in inches |
|---|---|---|
| Double-Crown .. .. .. .. | DC | 33 × 20 |
| Whole Imperial .. .. .. | I | 32 × 22½ |
| Large Whole Royal .. .. .. | LR | 26¾ × 20¾ |
| Large or Medium .. .. .. | L | 24 × 19 |
| Large Middle or Large Demy .. | LM | 23¾ × 18½ |
| Crown .. .. .. .. .. | C | 20 × 16¼ |
| Foolscap .. .. .. .. | FC | 18½ × 14½ |

## CLOTH

**BOOK CLOTH.** Book cloths in a wide variety of colours, textures and qualities are stocked in rolls which are about a yard wide and about 36 yds. long. Cloth can, however, usually be bought by the yard in the above width from most suppliers.

A careful selection should be made of cloths of good quality and colour. Some poor quality materials react badly to paste, they often stretch out of shape and the paste comes through the material and damages the surface. The best are waterproof on the surface and can, if necessary, be cleaned by means of a moist sponge.

ART CANVAS, ART VELLUM AND ART LINEN. Thick and strong materials and are used on good work particularly on large books.

LINEN BUCKRAM. Is very strong and stands up to hard wear in libraries and the like and is most suitable for large, heavy books. Cotton buckram is not as hard wearing as the linen variety.

MULL OR MUSLIN. Open wove material used for reinforcing the back and joints of books. Sold by the yard and is about 36″ wide.

## LEATHER

Acid-free leather should always be used for bookbinding of any value since even with only a slight trace of sulphuric acid left in it the leather rots rapidly. Avoid the use of any leather which imitates another.

MOROCCO. Undoubtedly the most useful leather for general purposes. It is made from goat skins. Average size of skins about 6 sq. ft.

LEVANT MOROCCO. South African or Cape goat skin. It is tough and hard wearing, is beautifully finished and has a large bold grain and is available in many colours. It is best used on large books.

NIGER MOROCCO. North African goat skin. It is native tanned by means of nut gall. Available only in a limited range of colours but is a very useful leather.

OASIS MOROCCO. Algerian goat skin, is the cheapest of the moroccos and the softest. Available in many colours.

## SHEEPSKINS

Used for cheaper bindings. Very often grained to imitate other leathers. Average size of skins, 7 sq. ft. to 10 sq. ft.

BASIL. Heavy skin tanned with vegetable dyestuffs. Used mainly for account books.

ROAN. Medium weight skin tanned with sumach and is a little softer than basil. Often grained to imitate morocco.

SKIVER. The grain side of split skin tanned with sumach. The strength value of skiver is small and it should be avoided.

FORRIL. Unsplit sheepskin which has been well stretched, chalked and pumiced.

PERSIAN. East Indian sheepskin. Fairly strong but is not recommended because of its lack of durability. Often imitates morocco or calf.

PARCHMENT. Sheepskin prepared like vellum, but the resulting material is not nearly so strong.

CALF. Wears well if properly tanned with oak bark or sumach. Available in attractive shades of colour, it is very soft and is quite thin and flexible but its strength is such that it should not be used on large books.

VELVET CALF. Calf with the grain side buffed off.

ROUGH CALF. Calf skin finished on the flesh side and used on books with the flesh side outermost. Often used on account books.

RUSSIA LEATHER. Cow and calf skins, originally made in Russia by tanning with birch bark. Now made here from large calf skins and given the characteristic Russia leather odour by treatment with birch tan oil.

VELLUM. Calf skin which has been soaked in lime, scraped and pumiced. It has a hard, smooth surface and is very strong and durable but is affected by variations of atmospheric heat and moisture.

PIGSKIN. Very hard wearing if well tanned. Natural coloured allumed skins are very strong but the dyed skins are liable to be inferior. The hard nature of the skin makes it most suitable for large books. Undue thinning of the leather by paring away the flesh side should be avoided as this greatly reduces its strength. Imitations of pigskin are very common, true skins have the hair-holes showing right through the leather whereas in the case of imitations the impressions are just stamped on the face side only and are not visible when the flesh side is inspected.

SEALSKIN. Newfoundland and Greenland seal skins. Excellent and hard wearing as a bookbinding leather. Soft and with a very even grain resembling that of morocco. It is considered to be the strongest of leathers.

## MISCELLANEOUS MATERIALS

TAPE. Unbleached linen tape, which has been stiffened, will be needed for sewing the sections of the book. Tape $\frac{1}{2}''$ wide will be found most generally useful but tape in $\frac{3}{8}''$ and $\frac{5}{8}''$ widths can be obtained if required. It is sold in coils of 12 yds. and 36 yds.

THREAD. Unbleached linen thread, called 16's 2-cord, is a useful thickness for all-round work; 25's 2-cord is thinner and may be needed occasionally. It is sold in reels containing $\frac{1}{2}$ oz. or 2 oz., and also in $\frac{1}{2}$ oz. skeins.

WAXED PAPER. Waxed paper is useful as waterproof sheets for use when pressing. Breakfast cereal boxes usually have sheets of a useful size.

**OILED BOARDS.** These are thin cards impregnated with oil to make them waterproof. They are available in sizes about 11″ by 8″ and 24″ by 19″ and are excellent for use as waterproof sheets when pressing—they last longer than the rather fragile waxed paper.

## ADHESIVES

**PASTE.** Paste made from ordinary flour is good, but paste made with cold water from prepared paste powder is much more convenient for general use.

**GLUE.** Scotch skin glue is sold by the pound in three common forms: as cakes about 6″ by 3″ by $\frac{1}{2}$″ thick; as pearl or grain about $\frac{3}{16}$″ diameter; and as a powder. The powder or pearl forms are the most convenient as they require much less soaking in cold water before melting.

# Chapter III

# BASIC OPERATIONS

**FOLDING.** The usual practice in folding paper is for the long side of the rectangle to be folded each time, i.e., the paper is folded over from right to left for the first fold as in fig. 2 (b), and from top to bottom for the second as shown by the dotted line in fig. 2 (c), and so on for each succeeding fold.

The folder, held in the right hand, is placed at approximately the centre of the long side of the paper, F in fig. 2 (a). The corner A is then lifted by the left hand and taken over

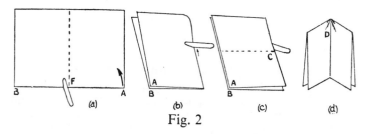

Fig. 2

until it exactly coincides with B and is there held firmly in place whilst the paper is creased along the middle with the folder as in fig. 2 (b). The fold is then slit with the folder to a point just beyond the centre, C in fig. 2 (c). If this is not done there is always the tendency for creases to form on the inside of the next fold as shown at D in fig. 2 (d). This is more and more likely to occur as the folds get thicker and thicker so that slitting should always be resorted to before making a second fold. The second fold is made at the dotted line in fig. 2 (c). The folder is placed at C and the top edge brought over so that it coincides with the bottom edge and the fold is then creased.

CUTTING. When cutting sheets of paper, rolls of cloth or boards, all cuts should be made right across the material as shown in fig. 3B. Although this may at first sight seem wasteful it will be found that if the pieces left over are carefully stored in a separate box they can be used up without difficulty. If projecting pieces are left on the main material they get damaged and bent and are thus rendered

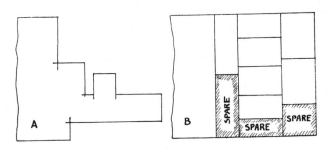

Fig. 3

useless. Quite often the over-cutting of the lines will also completely ruin the remaining piece, e.g., fig. 3A. It will be found that it is much quicker and easier to handle the material if the required pieces are first cut off the large sheets a little bigger than the finished size. The final exact trimming can then be conveniently done with small pieces which are much more easily handled.

Paper should be cut by first folding to rough size and then slitting with the folder, the trimming to exact size being done afterwards.

All pencil marks used to indicate the required size should always be placed on the reverse side of the material so that none is left showing on the face side to mar the appearance of the finished book.

Accurate cutting of cloth and paper should be done by means of a straight-edge and *sharp* knife. It is quite certain that much of the difficulty often found in cutting clean, straight edges can be overcome by using a really sharp knife.  Paper, due mainly to the presence of the mineral matter used in its manufacture, takes the edge off a knife very, very quickly and the oilstone should, therefore, be in continuous use and not just "once a month" as is all too frequently the case.

In cutting, *firm* pressure must be maintained on the straight-edge whilst several *light* strokes are made with the knife—the knife must not be forced heavily through the material but made to cut it cleanly by means of these light strokes with the *sharp*, repeat, *sharp* edge.  See plate VI.

The straight-edge should not be moved from its position until the scrap being cut off can all be pulled right away from the main piece.  If the straight-edge is removed *before* the cut is completely through the material at every point it is next to impossible to replace it in the identical position it occupied, this results in double cuts being made and a jagged edge being formed.

Cutting is best done on a sheet of stout strawboard and as far as possible the cuts should be made in parallel lines, starting at one edge and moving across the board using a fresh place each time.  If the cuts are made haphazardly across the strawboard in all directions it is soon impossible not to cut across a line already in the board.  This continual criss-crossing of the cuts on the board, besides making grooves in the board, also loosens little triangular pieces which fall out, the whole producing a very uneven surface on which to cut. This results in very ragged edges on the material since it

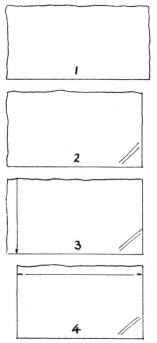

Fig. 4

does not bed down firmly on the strawboard when it is being cut.

The surface of an old cutting board can easily be renewed by gluing a piece of thin strawboard over the old cut surface and pressing.

CUTTING A PAIR OF BOARDS. If the following sequence is observed there should be no difficulty in producing a pair of identical rectangular boards, fig. 4.

1. Cut one edge straight.

2. From this true edge by means of a try-square mark off one end at right angles and cut to the line.

3. Mark the required length of the board along the straight edge and then square off at this mark and cut to the line.

4. Mark the required width of the board at each end, measuring from the true edge with a rule or by stepping off the distance with a pair of dividers. Cut off through these marks.

CUTTING A PAIR OF BOARDS WITH A CARD CUTTER   The cutting of a pair of boards or any number of identical pieces is simplified by the use of a card cutter. The following sequence should be employed, see fig. 5.

1. Cut one edge of each board straight.

2. Cut one end of each board at right angles to the straight edge. Mark this true corner.

3. Set the fence of the cutter to the required length of the board. When setting the fence of the cutter it is important that the distance of *both* ends of the fence from the cutting edge should be measured to ensure that the fence is parallel with it. Place the board with its true corner to the fence and its true edge against the ledge of the cutter and cut off the waste. Do this with all the pieces before moving the fence so that they are all identical in length.

4. Set the fence to the required width of the board. Place the board with its true edge against the fence and the true corner against the ledge and cut off the waste. Do this with all the pieces before moving the fence so that all the pieces are identical.

In cutting with the card cutter it is important that the board be held firmly against the ledge, or the fence, or both, for unless this is done the board is very liable to slip and so produce a cut which is not true.

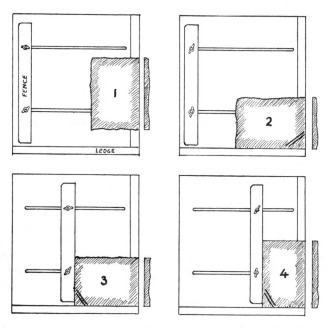

Fig. 5

If the card is thick and difficult to cut in the normal way, it will be found that little chopping motions of the blade will cut through quite thick card, but beware of straining the cutter by trying to cut material for which it was not intended.

SHARPENING A KNIFE. A knife used on paper or card is very quickly blunted and it is essential that the worker knows how to renew the edge. As the knife gets blunt

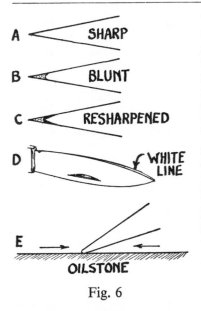

Fig. 6

the metal wears away and the edge becomes rounded off, fig. 6B. This is easily seen if the edge is inspected because the light is reflected off the rounded edge as a white line along the blunt section, fig. 6D. To sharpen the edge the metal must be rubbed away on each side until the rounded edge is removed, fig. 6C. This is done on an oilstone which has been lightly smeared with oil. Place the knife flat on the stone and then raise the back slightly so that the edge rests on the stone at an acute angle, fig. 6E.

Rub one side of the knife backwards and forwards on the stone a few times then reverse the knife and rub the other side. Keep rubbing alternate sides until a keen edge is obtained. Make sure that the white line of the blunt edge has completely disappeared before being satisfied that the knife is sharp.

SHARPENING A PLOUGH BLADE. The plough blade is sometimes ground to an arrow point and sometimes rounded off, fig. 7A and B—there is little to choose between these two shapes as far as efficiency goes. Spread a little oil on the oilstone and rub the bevelled side of the blade firmly backwards and forwards along the stone putting most pressure on the forward stroke. To find the correct angle at which the blade must be held, first rest the bevel on the stone, fig. 7C, and then lift the blade slightly to ensure that the edge is in contact with the face of the stone, fig. 7D.

When a burr can be felt on the flat side of the blade, fig. 7E, turn the blade over and lay it quite flat on the stone,

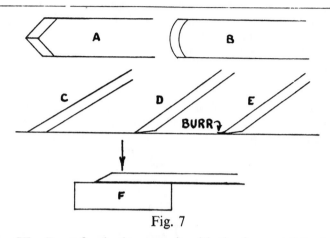

Fig. 7

fig. 7F. Press firmly downwards with the fingers of the left hand, as shown by the arrow in fig. 7F, so that the blade is kept perfectly flat on the stone and rub backwards and forwards until the burr is removed. Continue rubbing on the bevelled and flat surfaces alternately until the edge is quite sharp. Note that

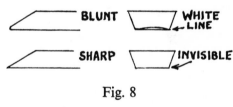

Fig. 8

it is the extreme end of the blade that does the cutting and it is this point which has to be sharp

Light reflects as a shiny white line off a blunt edge but a sharp edge cannot be seen when looked at end on, fig. 8.

Fig. 9

It is very important to remember that the flat side of the blade *must* be kept *flat* on the stone.  If the flat side becomes bevelled or "backed-off" it will not cut a true horizontal edge to the book since the cut will tend to rise with the bevel, fig. 9.

PASTING.  A supply of old newspapers is essential for use as waste for pasting upon.  Cut up the papers into single sheets of the required size—this should be rather larger than the sheets to be pasted.  Never paste upon a folded sheet of newspaper because it will be difficult to pick up the waste sheet and to discard it if it is still joined to the one

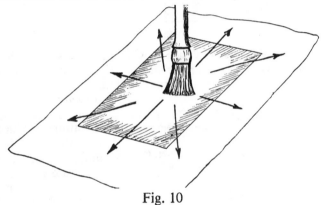

Fig. 10

below.  This rule of discarding the pasted waste sheet *immediately* must be rigorously observed—double the sheet up and place it in the wastepaper box—if this rule is not followed it is quite certain that a clean piece of material will be marred by being accidentally placed on the pasted surface of the waste sheet.  This discarding of the waste sheet *must* become automatic if clean work is to be produced.

Place the material to be pasted in the centre of the sheet of newspaper and hold it firmly in position with the fingers of the left hand.  Brush on the paste, fig. 10, working the brush from the centre of the sheet outwards, and carrying the brush well beyond the edge.  If this is not done there is a tendency for the brush to pick up the edge of the material and to bend it over as the brush is lifted and thus put paste on to the face side of the material. It is vital that the sheet being pasted should be held quite firmly and not allowed to slip. This slipping during pasting is by far the commonest cause of dirty work because the paste is picked up on the face side of the material from the pasted newspaper.

Pasting should be done quickly and with a large brush. A small brush is slow and allows the paste to remain too long on some parts of the material, thus causing it to stretch more than the parts of the material where the paste has been lying for a short time only. This uneven pasting and stretching causes distortion of the material and makes it difficult to handle successfully. The more "sloppy" the paste the more stretching will occur due to the water in the paste.

TIPPING. When "tipping", i.e., pasting a narrow strip along one edge of a sheet, a pasting guard is used to cover all except the strip. A pasting guard is quickly made by folding a piece of waste paper so that a straight folded

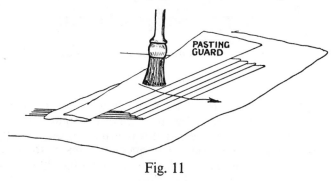

Fig. 11

edge is produced. A non-folded edge should not be used as it stretches and cockles badly as soon as the paste gets on to it and so allows paste to creep underneath the edge where it is not required. When several sheets have to be tipped they can be conveniently placed one on top of the other leaving only the strip to be pasted exposed and with a pasting guard protecting the top sheet. The paste is then applied to the whole lot at once by working the brush "down the steps" and away from the pasting guard, as shown in fig. 11, so as to avoid getting the paste underneath the edges.

After the tipped sheets are placed in position the book should be placed under a light weight until the paste is dry. The book should never be pressed as this would cause the neat, straight line of paste to be squeezed out into a broad uneven band.

**TURNING-IN AN OVERLAP.** When overlapping material is being turned in over the edge of a board it is very important that the board should be pressed down firmly with the left hand, as shown by the arrow fig. 12A. The overlap is then turned up with the folder so that it lies against the

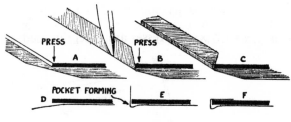

Fig. 12

edge of the board, B. The final drawing over of the material, C, is best done by the edge of the right hand.

If the board is not pressed down firmly before turning up the overlap a small pocket frequently forms at the edge of the board where the material is not drawn tightly against it, fig. 12D, E and F show how this occurs.

**HANDLING A LARGE PASTED SHEET.** The difficulty of handling a large pasted sheet so that it can be accurately placed in a required position can be overcome if the following procedure is adopted.

Pick up the sheet by two adjacent corners with the pasted side away from the worker and allow the remainder of the sheet to hang downwards. Swing the bottom of the sheet forward so that the unpasted side rests on the book. The edge being held can now be bent forward and placed exactly in position and held there whilst the rest of the sheet is unbent and rubbed down flat. See plate VII.

**RUBBING-DOWN.** Rubbing-down to make a sheet of cloth or paper adhere firmly should always be done through a sheet of *clean* waste paper. See plate VI. Rubbing directly on to the damp material may cause damage by rubbing away the surface or make it shiny by squashing the damp surface smooth with a folder or hard substance. Small creases can often be worked out by careful rubbing-down through paper with a folder.

Note that *clean* waste paper is emphasised, newspaper should *never* be used as the ink may strike off on to the surface of the material and so spoil it.

**PRESSING.** Two types of presses are generally used, an iron nipping press and a standing press.

The two plates of the nipping press are accurately finished and thus produce an even parallel pressure over the whole of the press surface. This ensures that the surfaces being pressed are brought into close contact over the whole of their area and are thus made to adhere everywhere.

The standing press is usually made of wood and has the main function of holding finished books flat while they are drying out, it is thus not essential that the press shall be so accurately flat as the nipping press.

Both presses have a central screw which transmits the pressure to the plates, it is thus essential that anything placed in the press shall be exactly central under the screw pillar, fig. 13A, otherwise the pressure on the book will be uneven as shown in fig. 13B. Damage will also be caused to the press if it is used in this way.

Pressing boards should always be used in pressing as the surface of the plates of the press may not be quite smooth and they also frequently collect small lumps of foreign matter underneath which would mark the surface of the material.

The material being pressed must be placed between sheets of clean waste paper for protection from staining. News-

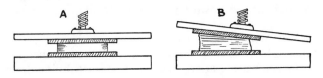

**Fig. 13**

paper should *never* be used when pressing because the damp material may be ruined by the print being transferred from the newspaper. Besides protecting the book the waste paper also prevents any excess paste or glue getting on to the press and the pressing boards.

NIPPING. Nipping, or the process of bringing the two surfaces being pressed into close contact, means exactly what it says, a "nip" and no more. The article to be pressed is placed between sheets of *clean* waste paper and then between pressing boards and placed centrally under the screw pillar of the nipping press. The press is screwed down tightly and then released *immediately*. This immediate removal is essential otherwise the great pressure exerted by the press will force the glue or paste right through the material and thus ruin it.

PREPARATION OF PASTE. The ready-made cold-water paste powders produce a very satisfactory paste which is easy to prepare.

Place a small quantity of water in a bowl and sprinkle the paste powder on to the water, stirring continuously with a flat stick or old ruler so as to prevent the formation of lumps. Keep adding the powder slowly until the paste is of the consistency of thick clotted-cream when it can be used immediately, but if the paste can be allowed to stand for a while it will improve its smooth consistency—ideally it should be left overnight. The paste can be made either thinner or thicker by adding more water or more paste powder as required.

Ordinary flour paste can be made by placing a small quantity of flour in a basin and adding cold water to it, stirring so that it is quite free from lumps. When it attains the consistency of thin cream place it in an enamelled saucepan and add double its volume of boiling water. Stir until the paste thickens and then boil for two minutes. When cool the paste can be thinned with cold water if it is too thick. A teaspoonful of alum added before boiling helps to preserve the paste.

For use the paste should be a thickish cream. If the paste is too thin the excess water is liable to stretch the paper or cloth badly, if too thick it will be difficult to spread evenly—the happy medium must be found by experience.

**PREPARATION OF GLUE.** The standard form of glue pot consisting of an inner vessel surrounded by an outer one containing water is essential for heating glue.

Cake glue should be broken up into small pieces and covered with cold water and allowed to soak for at least six hours until it absorbs as much water as it can—it is best left to soak overnight. It is then placed in the inner container of the glue pot and the water in the outer portion brought to the boil. The glue should now be thin enough to run off the brush in a thin stream without breaking into drops. This consistency is about right for use when gluing backs, or split boards, etc., but for gluing paper or cloth the glue should be quite thin.

Glue is also available in pearl or powder form. The pearl form needs soaking for two hours before heating. Add the pearls to the cold water, stirring continuously for two minutes and then occasionally afterwards and allow to soak for two hours. This stirring is essential to prevent the grains from sticking together in one solid mass and so greatly lengthening the necessary soaking time.

Powdered glue should be sprinkled into cold water and stirred and allowed to soak for one hour before heating. The note about stirring pearl glue applies equally strongly to the powdered form.  In emergency the powder may be added to water in the glue pot and heated immediately, again stirring well, but a period of soaking makes certain of a glue that is quite free from lumps.

# Chapter IV

# BINDING A SINGLE-SECTIONED BOOK

BEFORE starting to bind any book the first thing to decide upon is the style of binding, this involves the use of either paper, cloth or leather or a combination of these. Each of these materials can be had in a variety of colours and a very careful choice must be made before any work is started, so that the colours used will combine well on the finished book—not forgetting that the colour of the endpaper must also be taken into account.

The style of binding chosen in this case is "Half Cloth", i.e., it will have cloth on the back and corners and paper on the sides. A choice must therefore be made of cloth and paper of suitable colours for the cover together with an endpaper to match.

PREPARING THE ENDPAPERS. 1. Cut two white sheets and two coloured sheets of paper so that, when folded, they are about $\frac{1}{2}''$ longer and wider than the book.

2. Insert them one inside the other, as shown in fig. 14 so that a white is on the outside, then two coloured sheets, and then the last white on the inside of the coloured ones.

3. Trim one end of the endpapers square with the back fold and mark this true corner by means of a pencil mark across it as in figs. 14 and 15.

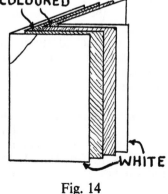

COLOURED

WHITE

Fig. 14

4. Remove the old sewing thread or metal clips from the book to be bound.

5. Insert the book into the centre of the endpapers so that the square corner of the endpapers is exactly level with the "head", i.e., the top, of the book as seen in fig. 15.

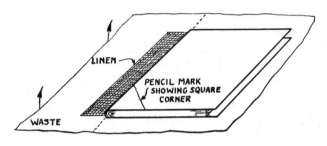

Fig. 15

6. Cut a strip of linen or old scrap cloth 2″ wide and $\frac{1}{2}$″ shorter than the length of the book.

7. Brush a *thin* coating of paste or glue on to the linen.

8. Place the linen strip, pasted side uppermost, on the centre of a piece of waste paper.

9. Place the back fold of the book on the linen so that 1″ i.e., one half, of the linen is covered as in fig. 15, and press down firmly. By lifting the waste paper as shown by the arrows in fig. 15, draw the remainder of the linen over on to the book and rub down well through the paper. Remove the waste paper and place the book on one side until the paste is dry. The linen need not be all in one piece, the required length could be built up from odd scraps 2″ wide butted edge to edge as suggested in fig. 17.

MARKING-UP FOR SEWING. 10. Make a mark on the spine of the book 1″ from the head and another 1″ from the tail and a third mark in the centre. Divide the remaining distance between them into equal spaces of 1″ to 1$\frac{1}{2}$″. These are now the points at which the stitches are to be made, fig. 16.

11. If the book is thick, make holes at these points with a fine awl so that the needle can enter easily. Make sure that the holes are made exactly through the back fold of the leaves of the book.

**SEWING A SINGLE-SECTIONED BOOK.** 12. Thread a needle with a medium thread and using it single, start sewing from the inside of the book. Fig. 16A shows the method of sewing for three holes. Push the needle from the inside to the outside at 1, leaving a tail of thread about 3″ long

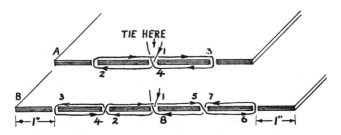

Fig. 16

on the inside. Pass the needle to the inside again at 2. Carry the thread right along the inside to hole 3 and push the needle through to the outside. Insert the needle again at the centre hole 4 and pull the thread through to the inside making quite certain that the original tail and the needle are one on either side of the long centre stitch. Pull the stitches tight and tie the ends *across* the long centre stitch. Cut off the excess thread leaving about $\frac{3}{8}$″ of a tail. A neat finish is obtained if the tails are frayed out with the point of the needle so as to produce a fluffy bow effect. Besides giving a neat appearance this is also functional as it prevents the tails from making little grooves in the paper when the book is pressed, see fig. 47C.

Sewing for five or more holes is similar except for the addition of extra stitches at each end and the sequence of the stitches should be clear from the diagram in fig. 16B.

13. Press the book between pressing boards for a while in order to settle the back fold firmly in shape.

**MARKING OUT FOR CUTTING THE FORE-EDGE.**   14. Make two marks on the side of the book at the head and tail at equal distances from the back fold, fig. 17.   This distance

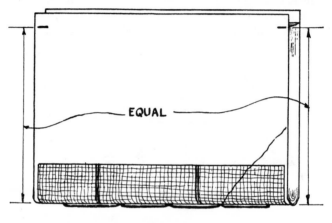

EQUAL

Fig. 17

should be exactly equal to the width of the pages of the book.   The distance is best measured by means of a pair of dividers but accurate measuring with a ruler is quite sufficient.

**CUTTING THE EDGES WITH THE PLOUGH.**   15. Provided that the book is quite thin it can be cut with the aid of a straight-edge and sharp knife, but thicker books need to be cut with the plough and press.   Place a piece of waste card at the back of the book to act as a cut-against and another at the front.   The front card, which should have its edge quite straight, is placed about $\frac{1}{16}''$ *below* the marks, i.e., allowing just the amount that is going to be cut off between

*PLATE VII*

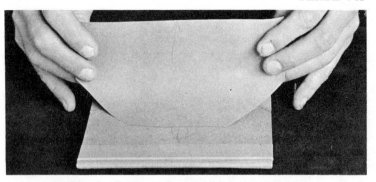

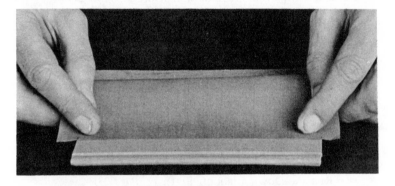

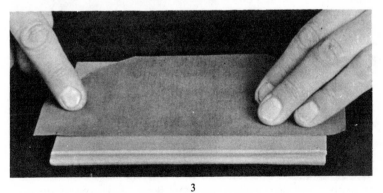

3
HANDLING A LARGE PASTED SHEET (*v. Page* 29)

*PLATE VI*

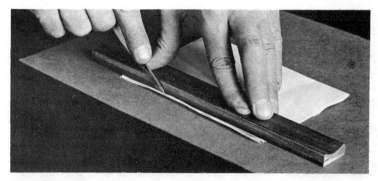

CUTTING WITH STRAIGHT-EDGE AND KNIFE (*v. Page* 21)

RUBBING-DOWN THROUGH PAPER (*v. Page* 29)

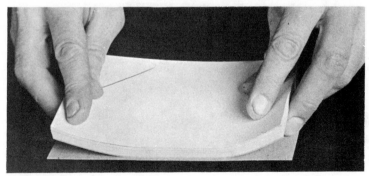

ATTACHING THE BOARD BY LAYING THE BOOK DOWN ON TO THE
GLUED BOARD (*v. Page* 38)

the marks and the edge of the card. Hold the cards firmly in place and lower the book into the cutting press and screw up until the book is gripped. By releasing the press a very little at a time the book can then be lowered, without the cards slipping, until the top edge of the front-card is exactly level with the cheek of the press, fig. 18. Screw the press up tightly keeping the jaws parallel with one another so that even pressure is applied all along the book.

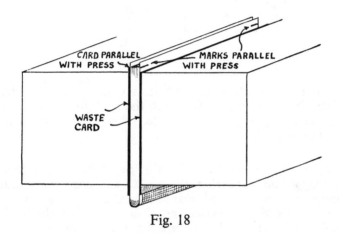

Fig. 18

16. See that the plough blade is *quite sharp* and then plough off the waste. Cut on the forward stroke only and advance the cutting edge by turning the screw only a very little each time. Attempting to cut through more than one or two sheets at a time inevitably leads to the tearing of the paper—as also does a blunt cutting edge.

**MARKING OUT FOR CUTTING HEAD AND TAIL.** 17. Square a line from the back fold across the head of the book just below the edge. This can be done with a try-square or by using the square corner of a piece of card as a guide, fig. 19A and B.

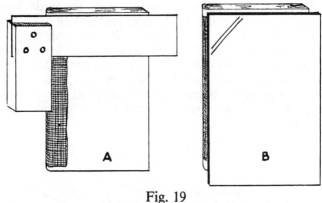

Fig. 19

18. Using waste cards, as when cutting the fore-edge, place the book in the press with the back fold nearest the worker and plough off the waste. Repeat the process for the tail of the book.

**PREPARING THE BOARDS.** 19. Cut two 1 lb. boards about $\frac{1}{2}$" longer and wider than the book. Cut one corner dead square and mark it. Then trim the other edges so that the finished board is $\frac{1}{4}$" *longer* and $\frac{1}{8}$" *narrower* than the book. Make sure that the boards are quite square otherwise the finished book will be out of true.

**ATTACHING THE BOARDS TO THE BOOK.** 20. Paste or thin glue one board. With the back of the book towards the worker hold the pages firmly together and lay the book down carefully on to the board, see plate VI; $\frac{1}{8}$" of the board should project at the fore-edge, the head and the tail as in fig. 20, and then press the book down firmly on to the board. This projection of the boards beyond the edges of the book is termed "the square", its function being to give protection to the pages of the book.

21. Paste or thin glue the other board and place the book down on to it as for the first board. It will be found easier

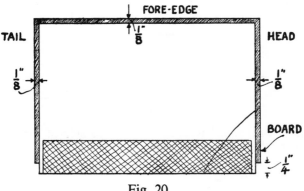

Fig. 20

if the top board is thrown back while doing this so as to obtain a better sight of the squares on the lower board.

22. Nip the book in the press between pressing boards.

**CUTTING PATTERNS FOR THE CLOTH BACK AND CORNERS.**

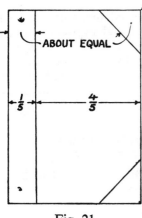

Fig. 21

23. Decide upon the width of the cloth back and the cloth corners by trial with paper patterns. There is no rule about these sizes but as a *rough guide* it is suggested that the cloth back should cover about one-fifth of the total width of the book. The corners should not be too large, their diagonal width being not greater than the width of the back, fig. 21. Cut paper patterns to the exact size required allowing ⅝″ extra for turning over the edges.

24. Cut one cloth back and four corners to the size of the paper patterns. The corners may be cut from squares or from strips as shown in fig. 22.

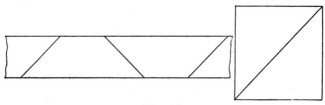

Fig. 22

25. Draw pencil lines on the reverse side of the cloth to indicate the position of the back fold and also the overlaps at the head and tail. Mark the overlap on the corners in the same way, fig. 23.

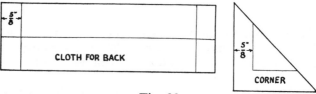

Fig. 23

26. The corners are always attached first. If the back were attached first it would be loosened by the continued opening and shutting of the covers while the corners were being fixed. Cut away the point of the right-angle of each corner-piece at an angle of 45 degrees leaving *slightly more* than the thickness of the board projecting beyond the marked position of the corner of the board as shown in fig. 24.

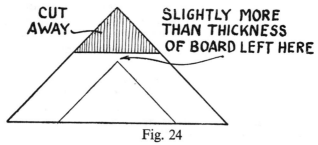

Fig. 24

27. Paste the corner-pieces and place them in position on the board level with the pencil marks, fig. 25A. Turn in the overlap at the head or tail *first*, then tuck in the little projection at the corner with the thumb-nail or folder,

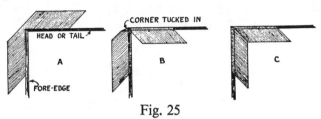

Fig. 25

fig. 25B, and then turn the overlap over the fore-edge, fig. 25C. When all four corners are attached wrap in clean paper and nip in the press. Note that in all covering operations in bookbinding, the head and tail overlaps are *always* turned in first and the fore-edge *last*.

**COVERING THE BACK.** 28. Paste the cloth for the back. Place the back of the book exactly on the centre pencil line,

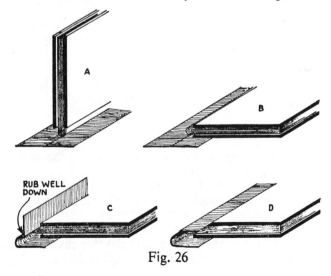

Fig. 26

fig. 26A, then lower the book on to one side of the cloth, fig. 26B.  Lift the other half of the cloth and rub down well on to the spine of the book and into the edge of the board with a folder, fig. 26C.  Then lower the remainder of the cloth on to the side of the board, fig. 26D.  Reverse the book and lift the cloth from the first board and rub well

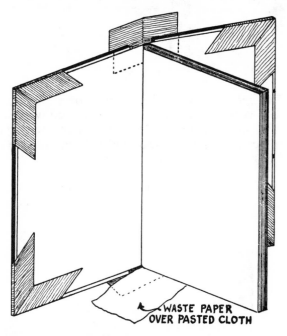

WASTE PAPER
OVER PASTED CLOTH

Fig. 27

down on to the spine and in to the edge of the board as before and then lower on to the side.

29.  Open both boards and place a scrap of waste paper on the pasted cloth projecting at the tail and stand the book upright on the bench as  shown in fig. 27.

30.  Place the edge of the hands on the top edge of the boards and turn in the overlap with the thumbs, the boards will have to be bent backwards slightly to do this.  Repeat

for the tail of the book and work the back neatly into shape with the folder. Wrap in clean paper and nip in the press.

**PREPARING THE SIDES.** 31. Make small marks on the cloth back and corners to indicate the position of the paper sides, which should overlap the cloth by about $\frac{1}{8}''$. Do this by measuring from the fore-edge with rule or dividers making the distances marked S in fig. 28A, exactly equal. Similarly make all the measurements marked C in fig. 28A exactly equal to ensure that all four corners will be the same size.

32. Cut two sheets of cover paper to overlap the boards at the head and the tail by $\frac{5}{8}''$ and also $\frac{5}{8}''$ wider than the distance from the marks on the cloth back to the fore-edge, i.e., S + $\frac{5}{8}''$ in fig. 28A.

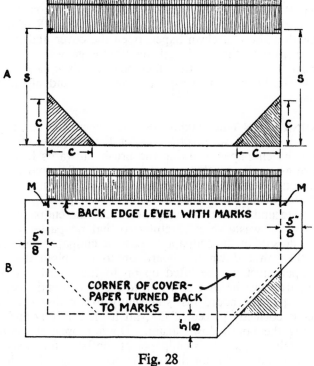

Fig. 28

33. Place the cover paper on the book with one straight edge level with the marks on the back and overlapping the boards equally at head and tail, fig. 28B. Now make small pencil marks, M in fig. 28B, on the paper exactly level with the edge of the boards at the head and tail; this enables the paper to be replaced in exactly the same position after pasting. Hold the paper firmly in place and turn back one corner so that the fold is exactly level with the marks on the cloth corner and then rub the fold in the paper well down, fig. 28B. Without moving the paper on the board repeat the process for the other corner.

34. Remove the cover paper from the book, lift the folded corner and place a straight-edge exactly up to the fold then cut away the waste with a sharp knife.

35. Paste the cover paper and place it on the board using the marks to locate it in its original position. Rub down through a sheet of clean paper, open the cover and turn in the overlap at the head, tail and fore-edge with a folder. Repeat the process for the other board. Place clean waste inside the boards and wrap in clean waste and nip in the press.

PASTING DOWN THE ENDPAPERS. 36. Open one cover and place a sheet of waste paper under the endpaper, fig. 29. Paste the endpaper, working the brush outwards from the centre as shown by the arrows in fig. 29. See that all the edges and the back are well pasted and make quite certain that the waste sheet does not slip during pasting and so get paste underneath the endpaper. Lift the endpaper and remove the waste sheet carefully so that no paste gets on the underside of the endpaper. Lay the endpaper flat again and then shut down the board on to it. Note that the endpaper must not be lifted up on to the board but that the board must be shut down on to the pasted endpaper.

37. Open the board just sufficiently to see that the end-paper is correctly placed, if not, lift it off carefully and try shutting the board down again. Do not open the board completely or the damp endpaper at the back fold may be stretched and it will not then return to its original position

without a pocket forming at the joint. When the endpaper is correctly placed, slip in a sheet of clean waste paper.

38. Repeat for the other endpaper and then nip in the press between clean papers.

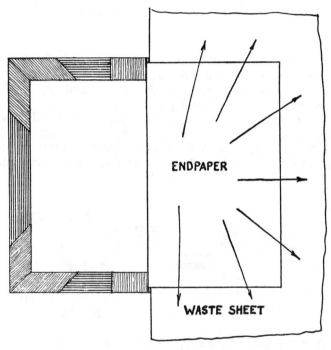

Fig. 29

39. Examine the endpapers by opening the boards slightly. Remove the waste sheet and leave the book over-night under a light weight and between pressing boards until it dries out.

**ALTERNATIVE ENDPAPER FOR SINGLE-SECTIONED BOOKS.** An alternative endpaper for a single-sectioned book can be made as shown in figs. 30, 31 and 32.

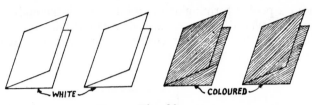

Fig. 30

Two folded white and two folded coloured sheets are required as before. Paste the whole of one white sheet and place one coloured sheet exactly on top and nip in the press, fig. 31. Allow it to dry under a light weight.

The term "made" is applied to two sheets which have been stuck together over the whole of their surface. Fold this "made" paper with the white inside and insert it into the other folded coloured sheet and insert the whole into the remaining folded white, fig. 32.

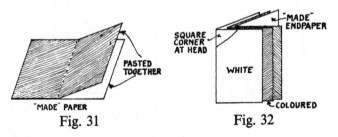

Fig. 31                    Fig. 32

Trim the head of the endpapers square with the back fold and proceed as before to line the outside sheet with a strip of linen and to sew the book.

**ALTERNATIVE STYLES OF BINDING FOR A SINGLE-SECTIONED BOOK.** The half-cloth style has been described. Alternatives are quarter-cloth, i.e., cloth back and paper sides; or full-cloth.

If a very strong binding is required split-boards made as described on page 96 could be used and the boards then covered in cloth or quarter, half or full leather.

## Chapter V

# PREPARING A MULTI-SECTIONED BOOK
# FOR REBINDING

1. Open the front cover and turn back the front flyleaf. Press firmly on the body of the book and pull back the first endpaper flyleaf, in the direction shown by the arrow in fig. 33, until the mull and the "slips", i.e., the tapes or cords, are visible at the hinge.

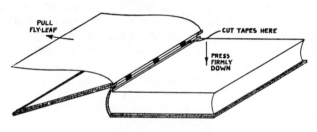

Fig. 33

2. Cut the slips and mull, carefully, with a sharp knife.

3. Repeat the process for the back board and the cover should then be free from the book.

4. Carefully remove as much as possible of the back lining without damaging the back of the sections.

5. When the book has a "tight" back, i.e., has the leather stuck directly to the back of the sections, the cover must be carefully pulled off the back of the book after first cutting the slips.

PULLING. 6. Turn over the first leaves of the book until the first stitches of sewing thread can be seen in the back fold of the section.

7. Cut *all* the stitches with a sharp knife.

8. Turn over an equal number of leaves when the "signature" should be seen at the bottom of the right-hand page indicating the first page of the next section.

SIGNATURES. 9. Signatures are the letters or figures printed below the text at the foot of the first page of each section. When letters are used, J, V and W are usually omitted from the alphabet. The first letter printed is usually B, the first section containing the title page, contents, etc., being un-lettered. When numbers are used the practice varies, sometimes the first section is not numbered and the text starts with 1, at other times the text is numbered 2. As the practice of printers in dealing with signatures is not standardised, each book should be examined carefully *before* commencing to pull it, so that the system of signatures is understood. If this book is examined it will be found that the first signature, B, indicating the first page of the second section, appears at the bottom right-hand side of page 5. The first section consisting of the title page, etc., bears no mark. The next signature, C, indicating the first page of the third section appears on page 21, and so on every 16 pages throughout the book.

10. Close the first section, grip it firmly with the left hand and pull it gently away from the book, taking great care to avoid tearing the paper at the back of the section. Pull in the direction shown by the arrow in fig. 33, and press down firmly with the right hand on the body of the book.

11. With the thumb and forefinger remove all the glue and thread from the back of the section, turn out all "dog-ears" and place the sections *face downwards* on the bench. Repeat for the succeeding sections, placing them on top of one another in their correct order as they are pulled.

PULLING TIGHT-BACKED BOOKS. 12. With tight-backed books this operation of pulling is sometimes not easy owing to the difficulty of completely removing the hard lining on the back. It is then best to place a piece of waste card on each side of the book—the old covers will do very well—and place it in a lying press with about ½″ of the book projecting. Soak the spine with thick paste and allow it to stand until the lining has softened.

13. Scrape the back of the book with a folder to remove as much as possible of the soft glue and lining. Using a very sharp knife cut the threads on the cords or tapes by cutting along the length of the bands, fig. 34, then remove

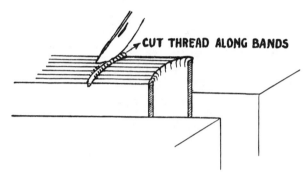

CUT THREAD ALONG BANDS

Fig. 34

the bands and scrape away the remaining waste. Some binders then proceed to separate the sections while the back is still damp, this has to be done extremely carefully to avoid tearing the soft, wet paper. Others prefer to allow the back to dry out thoroughly before pulling, in order to minimise the danger of tearing the sections. If the sections are damp, set them on one side carefully to prevent them from staining or from sticking to one another.

**KNOCKING OUT THE GROOVE.** 14. Knock out the groove, i.e., the turned-up back edge of each section, by placing it between a fold of clean paper and gently hammering along the back of the section on a knocking-down iron which is held firmly in the end of a lying press, fig. 35. Be careful to use the flat face of the hammer—if the edge strikes the paper it will easily cut a hole right through the section.

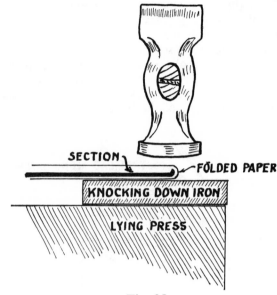

SECTION ⌐ FOLDED PAPER

KNOCKING DOWN IRON

LYING PRESS

Fig. 35

**PRESSING THE SECTIONS.** 15. Press the sections between pressing boards, putting a board or tin sheet between every five or six sections. See that all the sections are knocked up square and that they are all exactly underneath one another, fig. 36. Place in the press with the pile of sections exactly central under the screw pillar, as indicated by the arrow in fig. 36, to ensure even pressure, and press

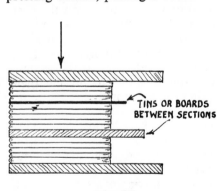

TINS OR BOARDS
BETWEEN SECTIONS

Fig. 36

for some time—overnight if it can be arranged.

New sections made by folding large sheets should always be pressed in this manner for as long as possible.

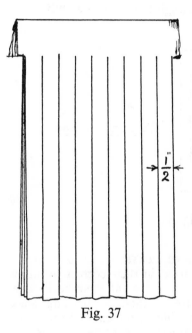

CUTTING GUARDS. 16. After pressing, all sections that are torn should be repaired. Cut strips of "bank" paper $\frac{1}{2}''$ wide and about $1\frac{1}{2}''$ longer than the sections. A convenient way of cutting a number of guards at once is first to fold up a sheet of bank paper several times. Then cut several strips $\frac{1}{2}''$ wide by cutting with a straight-edge and sharp knife right through all the thicknesses of the folded paper. By leaving the last $\frac{1}{2}''$ or so of each strip uncut the guards are all held together and can be torn off as required, fig. 37.

Fig. 37

MENDING TORN SECTIONS. 17. Paste the strip, the best way of doing this is to brush paste on to a paring stone or sheet of glass, place the mending strip on the paste and press down so that it picks up the paste. Lift the strip off and pinch each end together with the pasted side inwards, fig. 38. This prevents the strip from curling and so makes it easier to handle.

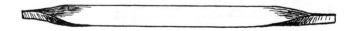

Fig. 38

18. Place the strip in the centre of a sheet of waste paper. Place the back of the damaged section exactly along the centre of the strip, fig. 39A.   Lift the sheet of waste paper and so draw the free half of the strip over on to the top of the section and rub down through the paper, fig. 39B.

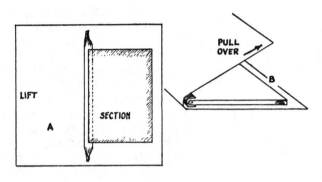

Fig. 39

**GUARDING SINGLE SHEETS AND PLATES.**   19. All single sheets and plates should be fixed in their correct positions either by tipping on with paste for $\frac{1}{8}''$ at their back edge, or preferably, by the far better method of guarding, since this enables the page to open right to the back of the book. This guarding is done in exactly the same way as the mending of a section, the plate being guarded to the appropriate section—the guard is always attached to the *back* of the plate, fig. 40.

Fig. 40

*PLATE VIII*

"COLLATING"—the sections are flipped over with the left thumb (*v. Page* 53)

*PLATE IX*

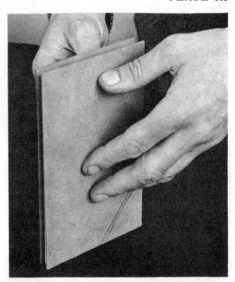

Knocking-up Square
at Head (*right*) and
Back (*below*)
(*v. Page* 54)

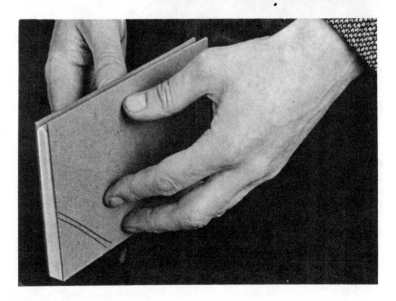

20. Allow the paste to dry out and then trim off the waste guards exactly level with the head and tail of the sections.

COLLATING. 20. Collate, i.e., check through to see that all the sections and plates are in their correct order in the book. This is most conveniently done if the sections, face upwards, are gripped by the right hand at the top right-hand corner, the folded edge of the separate sections can then be easily flipped over with the left thumb and the sequence of the signatures quickly checked. See plate VIII.

# Chapter VI

# CASE-BOUND BOOKS

THE term "case-binding" or "casing" is applied to that method of binding whereby the cover and the book are completed as separate units and the book fixed into its case as the final operation. This is the method used for nearly all the books now published and is done by machine except in the case of very small editions.

## CASED BOOK—ROUNDED AND BACKED

Style:—Cased in full cloth, therefore choose cloth and endpaper to match.

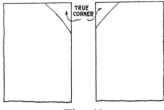

Fig. 41

1. Prepare the sections for rebinding, as described in Chapter V.

2. Cut two boards a little longer and wider than the book. Both boards should have one corner square with one straight edge and the true corner marked as in fig. 41.

**KNOCKING-UP SQUARE AT THE HEAD AND THE BACK.**

3. Place the boards one on each side of the sections with the true corner to the back and head of the book. Lift the book lightly between the hands and then drop the back and head alternately on to the bench so as to bring the back and head of all the sections exactly level with the true edges of the boards. See plate IX.

**MARKING-UP FOR SEWING ON TAPES.** 4. Place the book in the lying press with about $\frac{1}{2}''$ of the back projecting above the press, fig. 42. Check to see that the sections are quite level at the head and back.

5. The position of the tapes and kettle-stitches is squared across the back with a try-square and pencil, fig. 42. The term kettle-stitch is derived from the German word ketten-stich which means a chain stitch. For a small book two tapes will suffice; but for a book of the size of the average novel, three tapes are usual, the number of tapes being increased as the size of the book dictates.

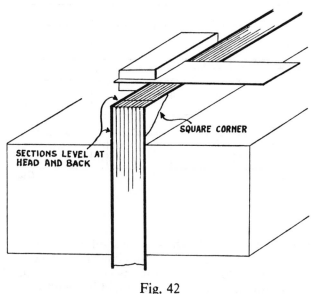

SQUARE CORNER

SECTIONS LEVEL AT
HEAD AND BACK

Fig. 42

6. The details of the marking-up are shown in fig. 43. First allow about ⅛″ at the head and tail—this allows for the trimming of the edges later—then divide the remaining distance into one more space than the number of tapes to be used, e.g., for *three* tapes mark out *four* spaces. Square lines across at these points, A, B, C. On the side of these lines nearest to the head of the book, square across other

lines X, Y, Z, $\frac{1}{2}''$ away, i.e., the usual width of the tapes used.    The kettle-stitch marks, K, K, are then squared across about $\frac{1}{2}''$ from the head and the tail.

7. Saw-in the kettle-stitch marks by just touching with a tenon saw so that the kerf produced is only of just sufficient depth to accommodate a double thickness of sewing thread.

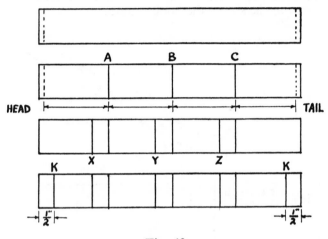

Fig. 43

Too deep a saw-cut will show as unsightly gaps inside the book after it is bound.    Some bookbinders also saw-in the tape marks in order to make the sewing a little easier, but this is very doubtful practice and should be avoided.

**SETTING UP THE SEWING FRAME.**    8. Remove the book from the press and place it *face downwards* on the sewing frame and set up the tapes to correspond with the marks on the book, fig. 44.

9. Turn the sections over so that they lie *face upwards* behind the sewing frame—after first collating to see that the sections are all in their correct order for sewing.

**SEWING THE SECTIONS ON TAPES.** 10. Open the first section at the middle, make quite certain that it *is* the middle, and then place it *face downwards* on the sewing frame with the head to the right and with the marks level with the tapes.

11. Sew with the thread single. The length of thread in the needle should be just long enough to handle comfortably—too long a thread is liable to get tangled and thus slow up the work. Fig. 45A shows the sequence of the stitches. Pass the needle from the outside to the inside of the section at the kettle-stitch mark at the head, 1, out at 2 at the *side* of the tape, across the front of the tape on the outside and then inside again at 3 by the *side* of the tape.

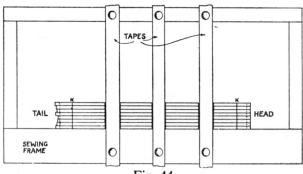

Fig. 44

Make quite certain that the thread does not go through the tape itself but only round the outside of it. Continue sewing in the same way at each tape to the end of the section when the thread will emerge at the kettle-stitch mark at the tail, 8. A short length of thread of about 2″ to 3″ should be left on the outside at the starting point, 1 in fig. 45A.

12. Open the second section at the *middle* and place it *face downwards* on the first and with the *head* exactly level with that of the first section.

13. Continue sewing as before, entering at the kettle-stitch mark at the tail of the second section and finally emerging at the kettle-stitch mark at the head. Draw the thread firmly, but not too tightly, and tie to the tail left

for the purpose at the head of the first section, fig. 45B. The tension on the thread should be such that it is just firmly tight and no more—there should be no strain at all on the thread. Cut off the excess tail but *not* the main sewing thread.

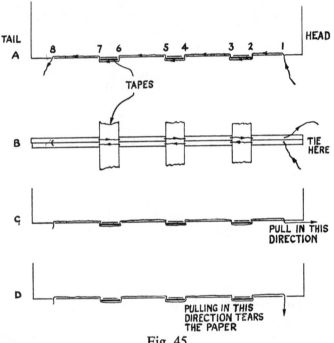

Fig. 45

14. When pulling the thread always pull along in the direction of the back fold of the section, fig. 45C. Pulling at right angles to the back fold will tear the thread through the paper, fig. 45D.

15. Place the third section in position with the head exactly level with the head of the first two sections. Enter the thread at the kettle-stitch mark, which is immediately above the knot just made, and finally emerge at the tail kettle-stitch mark.

**MAKING A KETTLE-STITCH.** 16. The actual kettle-stitch is now made for the first time, its purpose being to tie the third section to the one below. Pull the thread tight, insert the needle behind the stitch joining the first two sections, fig. 46A. Pull the thread through until only a small loop is left and then push the needle up through the loop, fig. 46B.

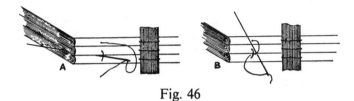

Fig. 46

Draw the thread upwards until the stitch is tight. This completes the kettle-stitch and links the sections to one another.

17. Continue sewing the book as for the third section and make a kettle-stitch *every time* the thread emerges at the head or tail kettle-stitch marks. Keep the *head* of every section exactly level with the ones below.

**JOINING THREAD.** 18. When a fresh length of thread has to be joined on, the knot should be so arranged that it lies inside the fold of the section and not on the outside where it might show as a lump under the cover.

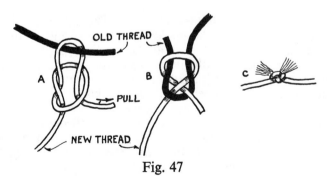

Fig. 47

19. The knot used to tie the thread is known as the "weaver's" knot—the common bowline—details of which are shown in fig. 47. Make a loop in the new thread as for a slip-knot, fig. 47A, and place the end of the old thread through this loop. Pull the tail of the new thread to produce the completed knot shown at fig. 47B. Pull the knot

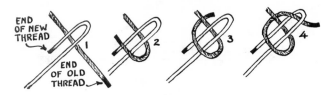

Fig. 48

tight—holding both tails—and cut off the waste leaving about ⅜″ of tail on each. If the point of the needle is now used to fray out these tails a very pleasant bow effect is produced, fig. 47C. This prevents the tails from making grooves in the paper when the book is pressed. An alternative way of making the same knot is shown in fig. 48.

**FINISHING OFF THE SEWING.** 20. After the last section has been sewn, finish off by making two or three kettle-stitches one below the other and cut off the excess thread leaving ⅜″ of tail.

**KNOCKING DOWN THE SWELLING.** 21. The increased thickness of the back of the book due to the strand of thread inside each section is known as the swelling. If this is only slight it can be left with advantage to the rounding process, but if excessive it must be reduced by slightly embedding the thread in the paper. To do this, knock up the book square at the back and head between the boards, with the tapes *outside* the boards. Hold the book firmly and lower it into the lying press so that only about 1″ of the book projects above the press and then screw up tightly, fig. 49. Hold the knocking-down iron, or other flat heavy weight,

firmly against the side of the book. Tap the other side of
the book gently with the hammer so that the swelling gets
beaten against the iron. Repeat with the iron held against
the opposite side of the book. The thread will now be
embedded in the paper and the swelling reduced. This will

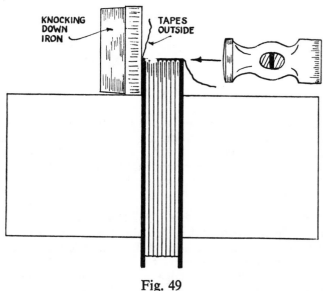

Fig. 49

cause the tapes to cockle up between the threads. Hold
*both* ends of each tape and pull it straight. Beware of
pulling one end of the tape only and pulling it right out—
the only cure for which is resewing the whole book.

PASTING-UP FIRST AND LAST SECTIONS. 22. This is necessary because otherwise, when the bound book is opened at
the junction between the first two or last two sections, a
rather large gap appears. Knock-up the book square at the
back and head and then throw back the first section. Fold
a piece of waste paper to produce a straight-edged pasting
guard and lay it on the book, leaving $\frac{1}{8}''$ of the second

section exposed at the back, fig. 50. Paste the exposed $\frac{1}{8}''$ strip—a little paste on the tip of the finger is the simplest way of doing this.

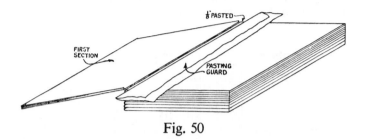

Fig. 50

23. Remove the pasting guard and turn the first section back into place and position it *exactly* level with the back and head of the book, fig. 51A. Deal with the last section similarly. It is very important that the back of the sections are exactly level and *not* as shown in fig. 51B.

**TIPPING-ON THE ENDPAPERS.** 24. Cut two sheets of end-paper which, when folded, are about $\frac{1}{4}''$ longer and wider than the book. Cut the head of the endpaper exactly square with the back fold and mark the true corner. If the book is to remain with uncut edges then the endpaper must be cut to exactly the same size as the book without any overlap.

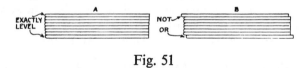

Fig. 51

25. Paste $\frac{1}{8}''$ of the back fold of the endpapers and place them in position on the book so that the head and the back are exactly level, fig. 51A. Do not press or the paste will be squeezed out into an uneven line, but place under a light weight to dry out.

**GLUING-UP THE BACK.** 26. The operations of cutting, rounding and backing, which follow the gluing-up, should all be done before the glue has set hard. Gluing-up should, therefore, *not* be started unless there is sufficient time also to cut, round and back the book while the glue is still soft.

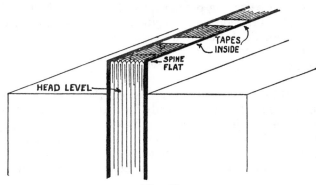

Fig. 52

Knock the book up square at the back and head between boards with the tapes *inside* the boards. Grip the book firmly and lower it into the lying press until about 1″ of the book projects above the face of the press, fig. 52.

27. Check to see that the back of the book is quite flat and the head level. This is very important as faulty work is inevitable if the sections are not correctly positioned before the glue is applied.

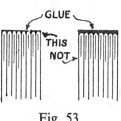

Fig. 53

28. Brush thin glue over the back of the book, working from the centre outwards, so that no glue runs down over the ends. Work the glue well in between the sections with a dabbing motion of the brush and finish off by rubbing the back of the book with the ball of the thumb. This removes any excess glue on the surface and ensures that the

glue lies between the sections and not in a thick layer across
the back as shown in fig. 53.   Too much glue on the back
makes the book difficult to open easily because when the
glue dries the back becomes stiff and is liable to crack.

29.  Immediately the gluing-up is completed, remove the
book from the press and take off the boards to prevent
them from becoming permanently stuck to the book.   Rest
the book on its side with the glued back just projecting over
the edge of the bench or a board, to allow the glue to dry.
See that the back of the book remains flat and does not
become distorted in any way whilst being moved.

**CUTTING THE FORE-EDGE.**   30.  When the glue just ceases
to be tacky the fore-edge is ready for cutting with the plough.

31.  Draw a line along the fore-edge of the endpaper
parallel with the back of the book.   Do this by stepping off
equal distances with the dividers at the head and tail,
fig. 54.   Draw identical lines on both the front and back

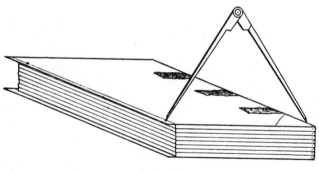

Fig. 54

endpapers, the distance of the line from the spine being
made exactly equal to the width of the leaves of the book.

32.  Place the straight edge of a piece of waste card level
with the line, and a cutting board also level with the line at
the back of the book.   Place the other cutting board on the
front parallel with, but just below, the marked line.   This

amount exposed below the line is the amount that is going to be cut off the book and it should always be as little as possible consistent with obtaining a clean edge, generally about $\frac{1}{16}$ of an inch should be sufficient.

33. Have the lying press only slightly open and, gripping the cutting boards and book firmly, lower them into the press until they become wedged. By opening the press a

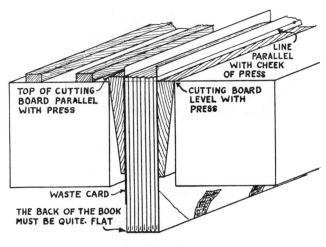

Fig. 55

very little at a time the book can then be lowered until the front cutting board is exactly level with the cheek of the press. The back cutting board should then be projecting above the press for the same distance as the pencil line on the front, since the back board is level with the line. Fig. 55 shows the book in its final position in the press. Look along the back of the book to see that it is quite flat and then screw the press up tightly, keeping the cheeks parallel with one another to ensure even pressure along the whole length of the book. Make a final check up to see that the book is correctly placed in the press otherwise the cutting will not produce a square book.

34. Sharpen the blade of the plough.

35. Refix the blade in the plough and test it to see that it just clears the face of the press and that it will run exactly parallel with the face. Should the blade not run parallel pack the front or back as required with a small piece of folded paper in order to bring it to a parallel position as shown in fig. 56B and D.

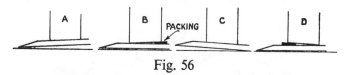

Fig. 56

36. Generally about 1″ of the blade should project from the plough, but if the book is thicker than 1″ then the blade must project an amount just greater than the thickness of the book.

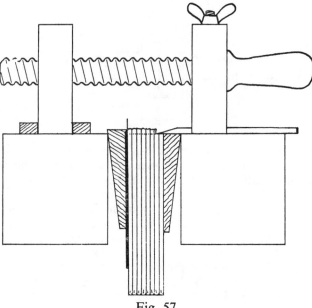

Fig. 57

37. Screw up the plough until the blade nearly touches the book. Hold the plough firmly downwards on the press and move it backwards and forwards, advancing the blade by turning the screw *very slightly* before each forward stroke. Little more than one sheet of paper should be cut with each forward stroke if tearing of the edge is to be avoided. Continue in this way until the whole of the edge is cut, fig. 57. Do not cut through the card at the back or the cutting board will be damaged.

ROUNDING THE BACK. 38. Immediately the cutting of the fore-edge is completed—and before the glue has set hard—the back of the book must be rounded. Place the book flat on the bench, press the ball of the left thumb against the fore-edge and pull on the side of the book with the fingers, fig. 58. This gives a slight rounding to the fore-

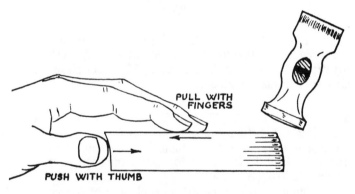

Fig. 58

edge. Tap the back lightly with a hammer to work it into shape. Turn the book over and repeat the process on the other side. Do this several times until the back is evenly curved and forms an arc of a circle, fig. 59A. A slight curve only is required, fig. 59B, C and D show faults likely to arise in rounding. Rounding is necessary to take up the

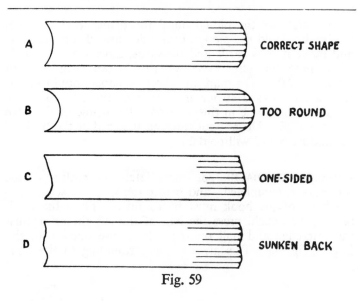

A      CORRECT SHAPE

B      TOO ROUND

C      ONE-SIDED

D      SUNKEN BACK

Fig. 59

swelling caused in the back of the book by the thickness of the threads and also to prevent the fore-edge from "starting" forward when the book is in use. Fig. 59D shows a fore-edge which has "started".

**BACKING THE BOOK. 39.** Backing is done immediately after rounding and before the glue has set hard. Backing produces a sharp groove into which the cover-boards fit snugly at the back and also helps to ensure that the back retains its rounded shape in use.

40. Place a backing board on each side of the book with the tapes *outside* the boards—there is a danger of their being damaged if left inside. The backing boards should lie parallel with the back and at a distance, equal to the thickness of the cover-boards to be used, away from the back fold, fig. 60, about $\frac{1}{8}''$ is generally required. If the backing boards tend to slip out of position they can be made to grip the book more firmly if they are slightly moistened on the inside.

41. Grip the boards and book firmly and lower them into the lying press until the backing boards are almost level with the cheeks of the press, fig. 60. Check to see that the boards are in their right position on the book and that the back has retained its slight curvature and then screw up the press tightly, keeping the cheeks parallel with one another

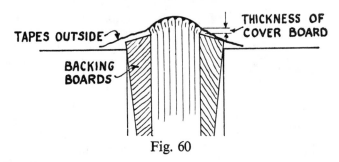

TAPES OUTSIDE

THICKNESS OF COVER BOARD

BACKING BOARDS

Fig. 60

so that an even pressure is exerted along the whole length of the book. If the book is not exactly right in the press the only cure is to take it out and reset it. This operation of backing fixes the shape of the back permanently and it is essential that it should be done accurately or good results cannot be expected.

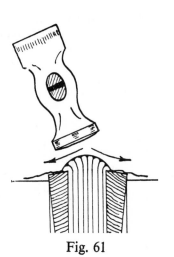

Fig. 61

42. The back of the book is now hammered lightly so as to fan out the sections evenly on each side, fig. 61. Start at the centre of the back and work towards the edges using glancing blows of the hammer as indicated by the arrows in

fig. 61. Gradually work the sections over on to each side as evenly as possible. The sides should finally be beaten down on to the backing board with the outside edge of the

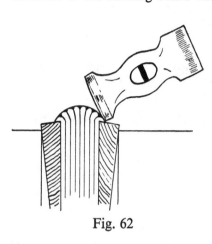

hammer as indicated in fig. 62. This produces a neat, sharp groove for the coverboard to fit into. Errors in backing are shown in fig. 63; A has the sections hammered over on to one side only making the book lop-sided; B has too high a back owing to the sections having been hammered on the sides only; C has had the sections crumpled by vertical blows with the hammer instead of the glancing blows indicated in fig. 61.

Fig. 62

**LINING-UP THE BACK WITH MULL** 43. When satisfied that the back is evenly shaped along its whole length remove the book from the press. Cut all tapes to the same length of about 1¼″. Place a piece of waste card on each side of the book up to the grooves, with the tapes *inside* the boards and place the book in the lying press with about 1″ projecting.

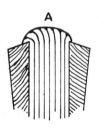
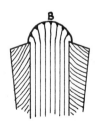
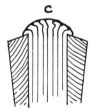

Fig. 63

44. Cut a strip of mull $\frac{1}{2}''$ shorter than the length of the spine and as wide as the back plus $2\frac{1}{2}''$, i.e., sufficient to overlap each side by $1\frac{1}{4}''$

45. Brush the back thinly with glue and place the mull centrally upon it, i.e., with $1\frac{1}{4}''$ overlapping each side of the

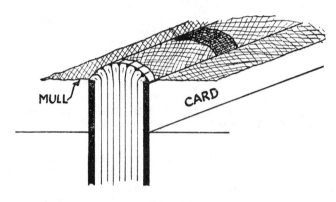

Fig. 64

back. Rub well down with the side of a folder so that the mull is made to adhere firmly all over the back, fig. 64. If the folder sticks it can be made to slide more easily if moistened with a little water.

LINING-UP THE BACK WITH PAPER. 46. Cut a piece of tough paper—brown paper does very well—the same width as the back and the same length as the book. While the book is still in the press for lining-up with mull, glue the back again and place the paper lining strip so that it exactly covers the back and rub well down with the folder so that it adheres firmly all over the spine.

CUTTING THE BOARDS TO SIZE. 47. Cut two boards exactly the same length as the pages of the book and place the boards in position on the book so that the true back edge

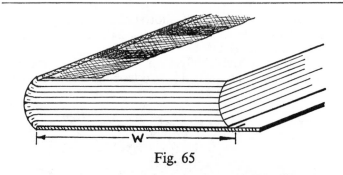

Fig. 65

is fitting closely up to the groove. Mark the width of the board ⅛″ wider than the pages of the book, i.e., as shown, W in fig. 65. Cut the boards to this mark.

CUTTING THE HEAD.    48. Place the two boards in position on the book and insert a

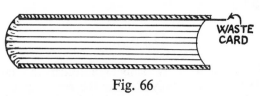

Fig. 66

piece of waste card, which has one corner cut square, between the back board and the book, fig. 66.

49. Knock up the book and boards square at the head and see that the boards lie exactly up to the grooves. Lower the front board a distance equal to the amount that is going to be cut off the head of the book, fig. 67.

50. Grip the boards and book firmly and lower into the lying press, with the spine of the book towards the worker, until the top of the front board is exactly level with the cheek of the press, fig. 68.    The boards must both be tight up against the groove to ensure that the head will be cut square. The back board should now be projecting above the press and parallel with it.    If it is not parallel, grip the lower part of the book and twist it between the fingers and thumb until it is correct, see that the front board does not move

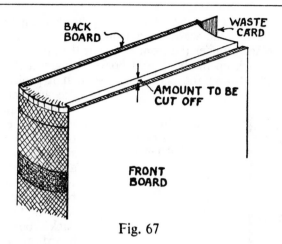

Fig. 67

in the process. The book *must* be correctly positioned or the cutting will be on the skew. Screw up the press tightly keeping the cheeks parallel.

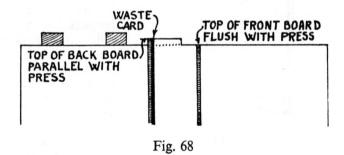

Fig. 68

51. Sharpen the plough blade and plough off the waste. Beware of cutting through the waste card and thus damaging the back board which has already been cut to the final size. Stop cutting at the waste card—the small portion still uncut which is formed by the back groove must be carefully cut away with a sharp knife.

**CUTTING THE TAIL.** 52. Remove the book from the press and take out the waste card from under the back board and replace it under the front board at the tail.

53. Knock up the book and boards square at the newly-cut head. Lower the back board so that it projects *twice* the amount of the required square below the head, fig. 69. These *two* squares projection are required because when the tail of the book is cut level with the tail of the back board, the boards are replaced in position. This will mean that the back board has to be raised from its position in fig. 69 so that one square projects above the tail of the book— thus reducing the projection at the head from two squares to one square. Set the book in the press exactly as for cutting the head and plough off the waste level with the tail of the back board.

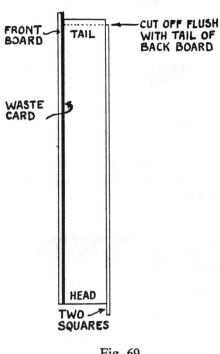

Fig. 69

**STICKING DOWN THE TAPES AND MULL.** 54. This is the final operation in making the book ready to receive its case. Lay the book on its side on the bench and using as little glue as possible first stick down the tapes to the endpaper and then the mull down on top of the tapes, working both the tapes and mull down into the grooves, fig. 65. Place the book on one side while the case is being made.

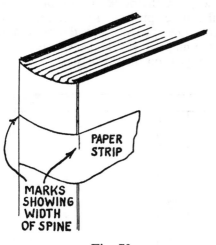

PAPER
STRIP

MARKS
SHOWING
WIDTH
OF SPINE

Fig. 70

MAKING A CASE. 55. Place the cover boards tight up to the grooves at the back. Wrap a strip of paper round the spine of the book and make a pencil-mark on the strip exactly level with the edge of the boards, fig. 70. The required width of lining-strip or hollow for the case is $\frac{1}{8}''$ *less* than shown by the marks.

56. Cut a strip of manilla or stiff paper to this reduced width and make its length exactly equal to the length of the boards—*not* the length of the book.

57. Cut a piece of cloth large enough to cover the book plus an overlap of $\frac{5}{8}''$ all round. Mark on the reverse side of the cloth the position of the boards and the lining strip in pencil as shown in fig. 71. Note that the boards are set $\frac{1}{8}''$ away from the lining strip.

58. Paste the whole of the cloth, place the lining strip in position and then place the boards $\frac{1}{8}''$ away on each side as in fig. 71, and rub well down.

59. Cut off the corners of the cloth at 45 degrees, allowing a little more than the thickness of the board between the cut and the corner of the board, as shown at A in fig. 71.

60. Turn in the overlap at the head and tail, tuck in the corner projections and then turn in the fore-edge and rub down.

61. Turn the case face up and rub down through paper and work the folder along the hinges. Nip in the press in clean paper.

62. Open the case and place the book in position on the lower board with equal squares projecting at the head, tail and fore-edge. Shut the other board on to the book and work the folder along the hinge to set the back into shape. Turn the book over and repeat on the other side.

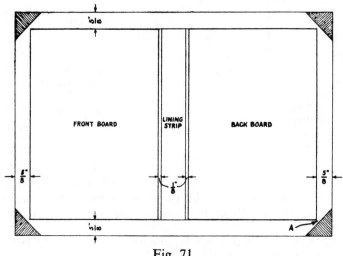

Fig. 71

63. Nip the book in the press with pressing boards set exactly up to the grooves, fig. 72. Remove from the press and leave under a light weight to dry out. Any lettering required on the case is most conveniently done at this stage once it is dry.

CASING THE BOOK. 64. Open the top board. See that the book is correctly placed on the lower board with the squares projecting evenly all round. Place a sheet of waste paper under the top endpaper, fig. 73. Paste the endpaper carefully, working the brush outwards from the centre. The left hand must press firmly down so as to prevent the waste paper from moving and so getting paste underneath the endpaper.

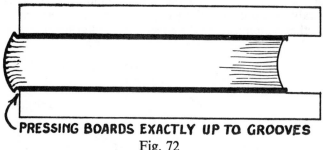

**PRESSING BOARDS EXACTLY UP TO GROOVES**

Fig. 72

65. *Lift* the endpaper and then remove the waste sheet. Lay the endpaper flat again and close down the top cover-board on to it carefully. Lift the board just sufficiently to see whether the endpaper is correctly positioned and then press the board down firmly. Do not open the board right back or the damp soft endpaper will stretch in the joint causing a pocket to form when the board is closed.

66. Turn the book over and paste down the other end-paper in the same way.

67. Open each board just sufficiently to slip in a sheet of clean waste paper under each endpaper and nip in the press between pressing boards set up to the grooves as in fig. 72. Remove from the press and examine the endpapers

Fig. 73

and then replace the book between pressing boards and leave under a light weight or in the standing press until quite dry.

### FLAT-BACK BOOK

The full process of rounding and backing a book has been described above but the method of binding can be considerably simplified if the back of the book is left flat. As a further simplification the edges may be left uncut.

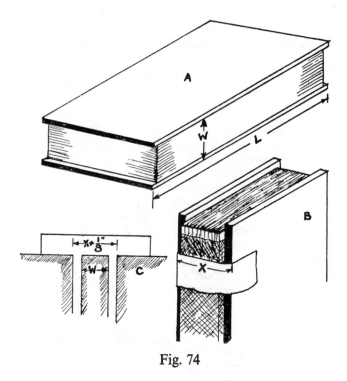

Fig. 74

Proceed as described above in paragraphs 1 to 37 and then cut the head and tail.

Line up the back with mull and paper, paragraphs 43 to 46, and stick down the mull and tapes on to the sides.

Cut the boards so that they are the same width as the book and overlap the head and tail by $\frac{1}{8}''$, fig. 74A.

**MAKING THE CASE.** Place the boards on the book so that they project $\frac{1}{8}''$ at the head, tail and fore-edge. Hold them firmly in place and wrap a strip of paper round the spine of the book, fig. 74B, and make a pencil mark exactly level with the edge of the boards. This measurement, plus $\frac{1}{8}''$, gives the distance apart that the boards have to be placed when making the case.

For the lining piece cut a strip of manilla or stiff paper the same length as the *boards* and equal in width to the thickness of the book plus one board, W in fig. 74A.

Proceed to make the case and fix in the book as before, the positioning of the lining piece and the boards is shown in fig. 74C.

## ROUND-BACK BOOK

The back of the book is rounded as described in paragraph 38 above, but it is not backed. Again the edges could be left uncut, if so required.

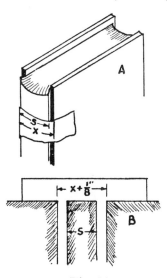

Fig. 75

Proceed as described above in paragraphs 1 to 37 and then cut the head and tail.

Round the back, paragraph 38. Line-up the back with mull and paper, paragraphs 43 to 46, and stick down the mull and tapes on to the sides.

Cut the boards so that they are the same width as the book and overlap the head and tail by $\frac{1}{8}''$.

**MAKING THE CASE.** Place the boards on the book so that they project $\frac{1}{8}''$ at the head, tail and fore-edge. Hold them firmly in position and wrap a strip of paper round the spine of the book, fig. 75A. Make pencil marks exactly level with the edges of the boards, X, and also mark the width of the spine of the book, S. The measurement from board to board, plus $\frac{1}{8}''$ gives the distance apart that the boards have to be placed in making the case. The width of the spine gives the width of the lining piece of manilla or stiff paper which must be cut the same length as the boards.

Proceed to make the case and fix the book into it as described before. Fig 75B shows the positioning of the lining piece and the boards in making the case.

# Chapter VII

# ENDPAPERS

THE endpapers of a cased book are usually folded sheets which are tipped on with paste. These are not strong enough for "bound" books, i.e., books which have their boards attached to them during the process of "forwarding" or the making of the book. Bound books have their cloth or leather covering added after the boards are attached to the book. This necessitates a form of endpaper which has a spare sheet on the outside to which the boards of the book are attached. These endpapers are sewn on outside the first and last sections of the book. There are numerous forms of suitable endpapers, the two commonest are described below.

To distinguish between the various sheets in the following description the folded sheet, one leaf of which is ultimately stuck down on to the board, is termed the "coloured" sheet, but this can be in practice, either white, coloured or patterned, as desired.

ZIG-ZAG ENDPAPERS. 1. Two complete endpapers are required, one for each end of the book. For each of these are needed one coloured and two white sheets which, when folded, are about $\frac{1}{2}''$ wider and longer than the book.

2. Take one white and lay a pasting guard along the back fold so that only $\frac{1}{8}''$ is exposed, fig. 76A. Folding the sheet of waste gives a good straight edge to the guard.

3. Paste the exposed $\frac{1}{8}''$ strip by working the brush off the guard as shown by the arrows in fig. 76A, this prevents the paste from getting underneath the edge of the guard.

4. Place the folded edge of the coloured sheet so that it just overlaps the $\frac{1}{8}''$ pasted strip of the white, fig. 76B. Nip in the press and allow to dry.

5. The top leaf of the white, marked 1 in fig. 76B, is now folded over on to the coloured sheet, fig. 76C. This is made easier if a crease is made in the white, tight against the fold of the coloured sheet, by running the folder along guided by a straight-edge, as in fig. 76B. Rub the fold down well with the folder.

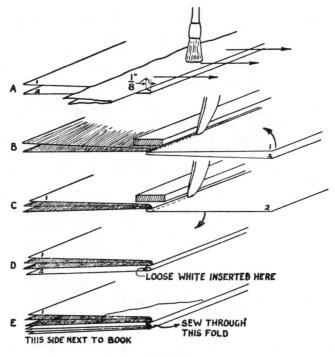

Fig. 76

6. The other white leaf is next folded back underneath the colour, as in fig. 76D, to produce the zigzag. Creasing with the folder as in fig. 76C enables the fold to be made more accurately when the paper is turned over.

7. Insert the other folded white, without pasting, into the half of the zigzag just formed and nip in the press.

8. Produce the endpaper for the other end in the same way. Be careful with patterned papers to see that the design will be the right way up at each end.

9. Trim off the head of each endpaper square with the back fold and mark the true corner on the outside of the waste sheet as in fig. 76E. Make certain that the single sheet of white is on the outside in each case and that the true corner is at the head.

10. These endpapers are sewn on with the sections of the book through the loose folded white as shown in fig. 76E, and *not* through the fold of the coloured sheet.

"MADE" ENDPAPERS. When two sheets of paper are pasted together over the whole of their surface they are termed "made". This type of endpaper has the advantage of giving a superior appearance since at the same opening of the endpaper a double white is seen and not one page white and the other coloured as is the case when the white and coloured leaves are not "made" together. Another advantage is that in the case of marbled endpapers the back of the marbled sheet is often stained and so by being "made" to the white the stained surface will be concealed.

1. One coloured and two white sheets are required for each endpaper. They should be, when folded, about $\frac{1}{2}''$ longer and wider than the book. Place them one inside the other and trim them all to the same size.

2. Paste the whole of the top surface of one folded white sheet, fig. 77A. It is *always* the white that is pasted so that the shrinking of the white in drying curls the "made" sheet towards the book and not away from it as would be the case if the coloured sheet were pasted. This is termed "drawing" towards the book.

3. Place the folded colour on top of the pasted white with the folds of each exactly level with one another, fig. 77B. Nip in the press and hang on a line or place on one side to dry for a few minutes.

4. Paste $\frac{1}{8}''$ of the folded edge of the other white with the aid of a pasting guard and place it on top of the first white with the fold exactly level with those of the other two,

fig. 77C.   Place under a light weight to dry out.   Do not
nip in the press or the $\frac{1}{8}''$ pasted strip will be squeezed out
into an uneven line.

5. When dry, the top white leaf, marked W in fig. 77C,
is folded back round the colour as in fig. 77D, and the fold
rubbed well down with the folder.   A nip in the press will
then settle the fold firmly.   The leaf marked W in fig. 77D
becomes the waste sheet and lies on the outside of the book.

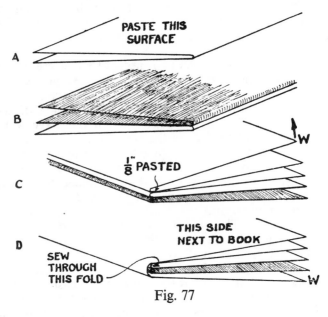

Fig. 77

6. Prepare the other endpaper in the same way, being
wary when using patterned papers to see that the design
comes the right way up at each end.

7. Trim off the head of each endpaper square with the
back fold and mark the square corner on the outside of
each waste sheet—make certain that the single white is on
the outside and that the true corner is at the head.

8. These endpapers are sewn on to the book with the
sections, the sewing thread passing through the folds of

the double white as shown in fig. 77D. Sometimes an extra folded white is inserted into this fold and the sewing done through all the whites in the same fold.

The "made" pair shown in fig. 77B are sometimes used as the endpaper for cased books. They are then tipped on with paste with the white next to the book.

CLOTH JOINTED ENDPAPERS. An endpaper which has a cloth strip at the back fold and which is attached to the book by sewing through the cloth joint, produces a very strong book that will stand up to hard wear. Various forms of cloth-jointed endpapers are in use, one simple type is described below.

1. One white or coloured sheet, as desired, and a strip of cloth $1\frac{1}{4}''$ wide and of the same length as the fold of the endpaper, are required for each endpaper. The paper, when folded, should be about $\frac{1}{2}''$ longer and wider than the book.

2. Paste, with the aid of a pasting guard, the reverse side of the cloth strip for a width of $\frac{3}{16}''$, fig. 78A.

3. Place the strip inside the folded endpaper so that the pasted edge is exactly up to the fold of the paper, fig. 78B. Nip.

4. When the paste is dry, $\frac{1}{4}''$ of the back edge of the endpaper containing the cloth strip must be folded over. Place the endpaper on the bench so that the face side of the cloth in the fold is uppermost. Make a crease with the aid of a straight-edge and folder $\frac{1}{4}''$ away from the back fold, fig. 78C. Press firmly down on the straight-edge and use the point of the folder to turn up the edge of the endpaper against it for the whole of its length, fig. 78D. Remove the straight-edge and rub down the fold, fig. 78E. Press for a short while to settle the fold.

5. Trim off the head of each endpaper square with the back fold.

6. Sew the endpaper to the book through the folded edge with the $\frac{1}{4}''$ folded strip next to the book, fig. 78F. If desired a loose folded sheet can be inserted into the endpaper and sewn through the same fold.

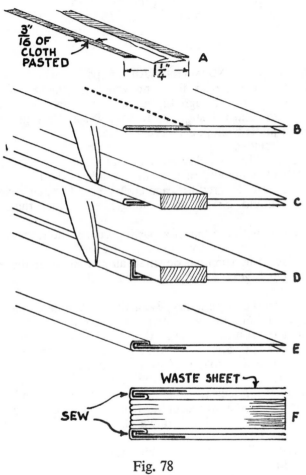

3"/16 OF CLOTH PASTED

1¼"

A

B

C

D

E

WASTE SHEET

SEW

F

Fig. 78

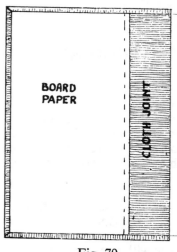

BOARD PAPER

CLOTH JOINT

Fig. 79

7. The outside sheet now forms the waste sheet to which the boards are attached.

8. After the boards are covered the back of the cloth joint is pasted or thin glued and the coverboard closed down on to it. This means that a further sheet is required to paste down on to the inside of the board. This single sheet is placed loosely in the pages of the book before it is cut so that the sheet is cut at the same time as the book and to the required size. The inside edge of this "board paper" will need to be trimmed down so as just to cover the edge of the cloth joint for $\frac{1}{8}''$, thus leaving about $\frac{3}{4}''$ exposed fig. 79.

# Chapter VIII

## HOLLOW-BACKED BINDING

THE preliminary operations in this style of binding are almost exactly as described for case binding. Details of similar operations will not be repeated here but the sequence of work is given with any slight variations added.

Style of binding—Quarter Cloth—i.e., cloth back and paper sides.

1. Prepare a pair of endpapers which have a waste sheet on the outside as described in the last chapter.

2. Prepare the sections for rebinding.

3. Cut the boards to rough size with one corner square.

4. Knock up square between boards—*omitting* the endpapers. See p. 97, section 8.

5. Mark-up for sewing on tapes.

6. Saw-in the kettle-stitch marks.

7. Replace the endpapers square at the head and back and mark the position of the tapes and kettle-stitches on them from those on the back of the book.

SEWING ON THE ENDPAPERS. 8. Set up the tapes on the sewing frame and sew the book, sewing on the endpapers as if they were the first and last sections of the book. Make certain that the single waste sheet is on the outside of the endpaper.

9. Knock down the swelling if it is excessive.

PASTING-UP THE ENDPAPERS. 10. Paste-up the first and last sections and also the endpapers for $\frac{1}{8}''$ along the back fold. Note the necessity of setting the back folds exactly level with the back and head of the book. See fig. 51.

11. Glue up the back.

12. Cut the fore-edge.

13. Round the back.

14. Back the book.

15. Line-up the back with mull.

16. Cut the boards to the exact size of the book, making them equal in length to the pages and $\frac{1}{8}''$ wider than from the groove to the fore-edge which is already cut.

17. Cut the head and tail of the book.

18. Stick down the tapes and mull on to the outside of the waste sheet.

**ATTACHING THE BOARDS TO THE BOOK.** 19. Thin glue or paste the board and, holding the book closed, lay it down on to the board so that the square projects evenly all round the fore-edge, head and tail, fig. 80 and plate X. Attach

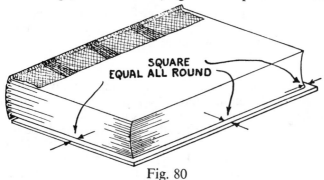

Fig. 80

the other board in the same way and nip in the press. If the boards are glued the book may be worked on fairly soon, but if pasted sufficient time must be allowed for the book to dry under a light weight.

**ATTACHING THE HOLLOW BACK.** 20. The hollow back is next fitted. Cut a sheet of brown or any stiff paper the same length as the *boards* and of a width equal to three times the width of the spine of the book from groove to groove. Obtain this width by wrapping a strip of paper round the back of the book and marking on it the position of the edge of the groove on each side, see S in fig. 75A.

21. Fold the paper for the hollow exactly into three, fig. 81A. Fold over one flap and place a sheet of waste paper underneath it and thinly glue the flap, fig. 81B. Remove

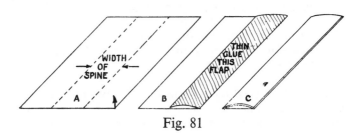

Fig. 81

the waste paper and turn the other flap over on to the glued surface and rub down, fig. 81C. This produces a hollow tube having two thicknesses of paper on one side and one thickness on the other.

22. Place a piece of waste card up to the groove on each side of the book and place it in the lying press with about 1″ of the back of the book projecting. The hollow will stick down more easily at the edges if it is first bent to the shape of the spine with the fingers or worked to shape over a round bar of about the size of a broom handle. Thinly glue the back of the book and place the hollow on to it with the *single* thickness next to the spine. Position the hollow exactly level with the edges of the groove and over-lapping the head and the tail equally, this overlap is seen in fig. 84. Rub well down with the folder so that the hollow is firmly attached all over the spine and allow to dry.

SLITTING. 23. The hollow and also the mull in the hinge at the head and tail must now be slit to allow the cloth to be turned in over the back. Open the boards and slit the edges of the hollow for about 1″ at the head and tail, fig. 82. Cut away the projection of the hollow on the inside, i.e., the single thickness, so that it is exactly level with the head and tail of the book. Slit also the mull at the edge of each

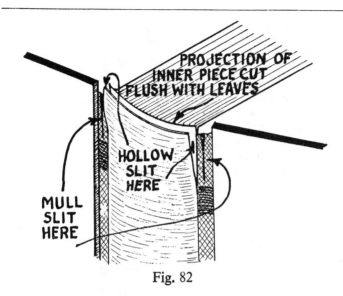

Fig. 82

board for 1″. Care must be taken not to cut either the thread at the kettle-stitch or the tapes. The book is now ready for covering.

**COVERING THE HOLLOW-BACKED BOOK.** 24. Cut the cloth for the back from a paper pattern, allowing $\frac{5}{8}''$ overlap at the head and tail and sufficient width to cover the back and

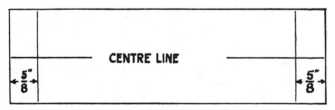

Fig. 83

to overlap on to the sides for about $\frac{1}{8}$ of the width of the board.

25. Draw a centre line on the reverse side of the cloth and also mark the overlap at the head and tail, fig. 83.

26. Make a mark on the inside centre of the hollow attached to the book at the head and tail, fig. 84.

27. Paste the cloth and lay the back of the book on to it so that the centre marks on the hollow at the head and tail exactly correspond with the centre line on the

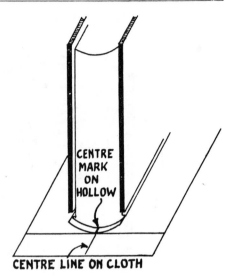

Fig. 84

cloth and let the overlap project equally at head and tail, fig. 84.

28. Press the back of the book down on to the cloth to make it stick and then lift the book with the cloth adhering to it.

29. Lay the book on its side with the back projecting over the edge of the bench and rub the cloth well down on to the spine. Work the cloth into the groove with the folder, fig. 85, and then lay the remainder of the cloth down on to the side of the book

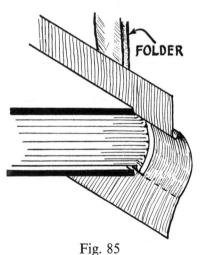

Fig. 85

and rub down. Turn the book over and repeat the process on the other side.

30. Open the covers and place a piece of waste paper over the pasted cloth projecting at the tail to prevent the paste from getting on to the edges of the book. Stand the book upright on the bench with the fore-edge to the front. See fig. 100.

31. Turn in the cloth over the hollow back and down into the slits in the mull and then over the edges of the boards, fig. 86. Turn the book upside down and repeat the

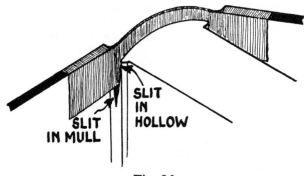

Fig. 86

turning in of the cloth at the tail. Work the head and tail carefully into shape with the folder in order to rub down any small creases.

32. Work the folder along the groove once more—very gently or the point of the folder may penetrate the damp cloth. Nip the book in the press with pressing boards placed exactly up to the grooves. See fig. 72. Do not press the spine.

**SIDING A QUARTER-BOUND BOOK.** 33. Make small marks on the cloth $\frac{1}{8}''$ from the edge at the head and tail, fig. 87. It is better to measure from the fore-edge of the boards to ensure that the cloth left exposed is parallel all the way down the book. Dividers set to the required distance make

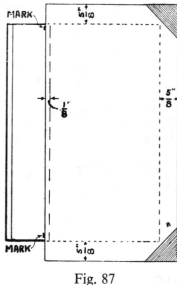

Fig. 87

the operation easy and ensure that all the measurements on back and front boards are identical.

34. The paper sides are next cut long enough to overlap the head and tail by $\frac{5}{8}''$ and also $\frac{5}{8}''$ wider than the distance stepped out on the boards, i.e., from mark to fore-edge, fig. 87.

35. Paste the paper and lay it on to the boards up to the marks with an equal overlap at head and tail and rub well down through paper.

36. Open the board and cut off the corners of the paper for the mitre, i.e., the shaded portions in fig. 87.

37. Support the open board on pressing boards as shown

Fig. 88

in fig. 88, and turn in the overlap at head and tail first, then tuck in the corners and turn in the fore-edge last. Nip.

**PASTING-DOWN ENDPAPERS.** "Pasting-down shut" is the term applied to the method whereby the endpapers of all tape-sewn books are fixed. It means that the endpapers are pasted and the cover-board shut down on to them, as opposed to the method of "pasting-down open" used for cord-sewn books.

38. Open one cover and place a sheet of waste paper under the endpaper. Paste the endpaper all over, being very careful to see that all the edges are pasted as well as all along the back fold.

39. Lift the endpaper with a folder and remove the waste sheet. Lay the endpaper flat again and then carefully *close down the cover-board* on to it. Open the board slightly to see if the endpaper is correctly placed, if not, pull the end-paper off gently and try again. When correct press the board down firmly and repeat for the other endpaper.

40. Slip a sheet of clean paper under each endpaper and nip in the press with the pressing boards placed up to the grooves.

41. Inspect the endpapers by opening the boards for a few inches only. Do not open them right back or the damp endpaper at the joint may stretch and so form a pocket when the board is closed again.

42. Slip a sheet of clean waste under each endpaper and leave the book under pressing boards and a light weight until dry—overnight at least.

# Chapter IX

# LIBRARY STYLE BINDING

THIS style of binding, half leather, is extremely strong, it has leather at the back and corners and cloth sides. The tapes are inserted into split-boards and the leather is stuck directly to the spine of the book, i.e., it is "tight-backed".

MAKING SPLIT-BOARDS. 1. Cut two 1-lb. boards and also two ½-lb. strawboards each about 1″ longer and wider than the book. Glue the *thin* board except for a strip 2″ wide down one edge, fig. 89, using a guard of waste card or paper to cover this strip. Place a thick board exactly on top and nip in the press. Stand the split-boards on one side to dry out.

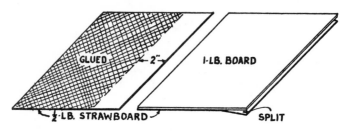

Fig. 89

The next operations are almost identical with those already described in detail for the case-binding in Chapter VI. The sequence of operations only will therefore be repeated here together with any slight additions

2. Prepare a pair of endpapers which have a waste sheet on the outside as described in Chapter VII.

3. Prepare the sections for rebinding, see Chapter V.

4. Cut two waste boards, with one corner square, to the rough size of the book.

5. Knock up the sections square between boards—*omitting* the endpapers. Place in the lying press with 1″ projecting.

6. Mark-up for sewing on tapes. Not less than four tapes should be used for a book of the size of the normal novel.

7. Saw-in the kettle-stitch marks.

8. Replace the endpapers square at the head and back and mark the position of the tapes and kettle-stitches on them from those on the book. The endpapers were omitted in the first marking-up in order to avoid sawing into them at the kettle-stitch marks and so producing unsightly holes on the inside of the fold when the finished book is opened.

9. Set up the tapes to correspond with the marks and sew the book, sewing on the endpapers as if they were the first and last sections.

10. Knock down the swelling if it is excessive—a slight swelling is advantageous in producing a good shape to the back of the book.

11. Paste up the first and last sections and also the endpapers for $\frac{1}{8}$″. With large books the first *two* and last *two* sections should be pasted up.

12. Glue-up the back.

13. Cut the fore-edge.

14. Round the back.

15. Back the book.

16. Line-up the back with mull.

17. Cut the split-boards to size. Make them exactly the same length as the book from head to tail and the same width as the book from groove to fore-edge. See that the "split" is next to the groove and that the thin board is on the *inside* next to the book. Mark the boards as at B in fig. 90, so that they can be replaced in their correct position when required.

18. Cut the head and tail of the book.

19. Stick down the tapes and mull on to the outside of the waste sheets. Allow to dry.

**ALLOWANCE FOR THE FRENCH GROOVE.** 20. When the boards are now placed on the book so that a square of $\frac{1}{8}''$ projects at the fore-edge a "French Groove" $\frac{1}{8}''$ wide will be formed at the joint. This is wide enough for a cloth back but due to the extra thickness of leather there would be insufficient room in the hinge and the boards would be

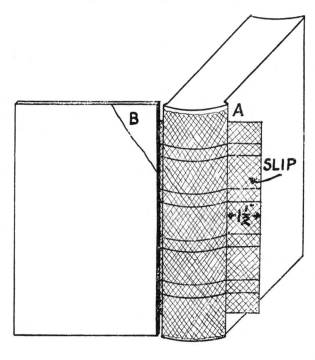

Fig. 90

prevented from opening more than a little way. Therefore for a leather back $\frac{1}{8}''$ must be trimmed off the edge of each board in order to increase the width of the French groove to at least $\frac{1}{4}''$. The final width of the boards is now $\frac{1}{8}''$ less than the width of the book from groove to fore-edge.

**PREPARING THE SLIPS.** 21. Cut off the waste sheet, to which the tapes and mull are stuck, so that a slip of $1\frac{1}{4}''$ to $1\frac{1}{2}''$ wide is left at the hinge, fig. 90. This is the slip that is inserted into the split-board. In order to allow for the turning-in of the leather at the back, cut away $\frac{3}{4}''$ of the slip at the head and tail, as at A in fig. 90. Care should be taken not to cut the sewing thread or the tapes.

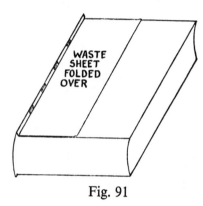

WASTE SHEET FOLDED OVER

Fig. 91

An alternative method of preparing the slip is to paste or thin glue the whole of the waste sheet and then fold it back on itself so that the fore-edge of the sheet lies along the groove and covers the tapes and the mull, fig. 91. Nip in the press between boards and cut to size as described above. This method has the advantage of making the slip quite stiff and so making its insertion into the split-board a little easier but has the disadvantage of producing extra thickness in the split which some binders consider clumsy.

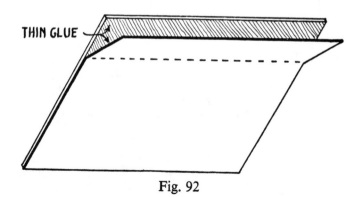

THIN GLUE

Fig. 92

**ATTACHING THE SPLIT-BOARDS.** 22. The split boards have now to be fixed to the book. Open the split and thin glue *both* the inside surfaces carefully, fig. 92. Insert the slip

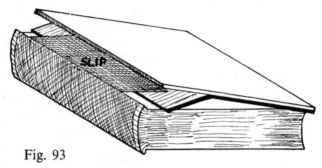

Fig. 93

into the split, fig. 93, adjust the squares accurately at the head, tail and fore-edge so that they are exactly equal and press the split firmly down, fig. 94. Repeat for the other

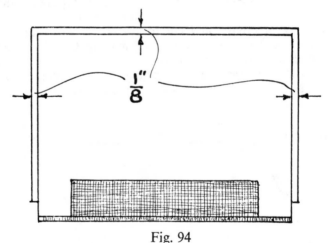

Fig. 94

board. Place a sheet of tin or thin board under each cover-board and place pressing boards on the outside level with the back edge of the boards. Place in the press for some

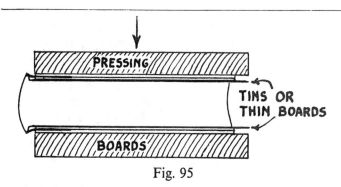

Fig. 95

time. See that the screw of the press is exactly over the centre of the book as indicated by the arrow in fig. 95. This ensures that even pressure is exerted on the book.

**PREPARING THE LEATHER FOR THE BACK AND CORNERS.**
23. Prepare paper patterns for the leather back and corners allowing $\frac{3}{4}''$ extra for the turn-in over the edge of the boards. Cut the leather to the size of the paper patterns. See p. 39.

**PARING THE LEATHER.** 24. Unless the leather is very thin the edges will now require paring in order to make them thin enough to turn neatly over the edges of the board. Mark the position of the back of the book on the reverse side of the leather with a soft pencil as shown by the dotted lines in fig. 96. The overlap of $\frac{3}{4}''$ at the head and tail must be pared back to just inside the line. The edges of the leather at the sides which lie on top of the board need only be pared for $\frac{1}{4}''$. The pared areas are shown by the shaded portions of fig. 96. To allow for the double thickness of leather produced where the turn-in occurs over the spine, the back must be pared a little lower as at A and B in fig. 96. The top edge of the leather, C and D in fig. 96, must also be pared to a clean feather-edge so that no ridge will be formed across the spine when the overlap is turned in.
25. Paring is best done on a lithographic stone or a sheet of plate glass. Hold the leather, face downwards, on the

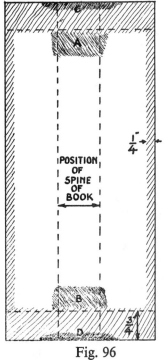

Fig. 96

stone with the left hand. Use the fingers to keep the leather flat and press it with the left thumb against the edge of the stone to prevent the leather from moving. Lay the blade of the knife almost flat on the leather with the fore-finger on top and well down towards the cutting edge. The knuckles underneath the knife should never be allowed to move forward over the edge of the stone otherwise the knife would be raised to too steep an angle. A steady downward pressure with the knife, which is pushed along by the fore-finger of the left hand, then removes a shaving from the edge of the leather. See plate X. Considerable practice is needed before this operation can be performed successfully.

26. The paring must be quite even in width and without any ridges since any unevenness on the under side will be seen on the surface of the leather when it is pasted down on to the board. When the shavings are cut off make quite certain that none get underneath the leather during the paring process otherwise a hole will be cut in the leather when the knife meets the lump caused by the scrap underneath. Test the paring by folding over the pared edge of the leather when any unevenness will be apparent. Frequent stropping of the knife will be necessary in order to keep the edge quite sharp, for unless the knife is in perfect condition the paring process is made extremely difficult.

**PARING THE CORNERS.** 27. Mark the position of the board on the reverse side of the leather, as shown by the dotted line in fig. 97 and pare the whole of the overlap to just

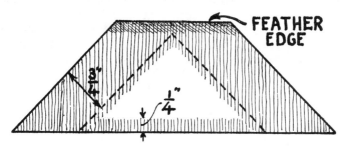

Fig. 97

inside the line. The front edge requires paring for $\frac{1}{4}''$ only. The corner which has been cut away for the mitre must be pared to a clean feather-edge so that the turn-in at the corner can be made neatly.

**PASTING THE LEATHER.** 28. First damp the face side of the leather evenly all over with a little clean water and a sponge or pad of cotton wool. Besides making the leather soft and easily workable, this damp surface prevents the face of the leather from developing "tide-marks" which might be produced on a dry surface by the moisture from the paste soaking through from the underside of the leather in places which happen to be thinner or more porous than others.

29. Lay the leather on a clean surface and paste it thoroughly, working the paste well into the pores of the leather. Fold the back double, pasted side inwards, and place the corners together in pairs, also with their pasted sides together, and allow the paste to soak in for ten minutes. This placing together of the pasted surfaces prevents the paste from drying out during the soaking process.

**ATTACHING THE LEATHER CORNERS.** 30. If the back is put on first it will, if still damp, be disturbed during the fixing of the corners and so to prevent this happening the corners are always fitted first.  Repaste the leather for the corners and remove all excess paste from the surface—it is the paste that has been worked into the pores of the leather that does the sticking.  Place the corner accurately in position and throw back the board on to pressing boards, as shown in fig. 98, so that the board lies horizontally on them.  Press down the board on to the leather and turn up the overlap with the folder.  Always turn the head or tail up first and the fore-edge last.  Tap the leather firmly against the edge

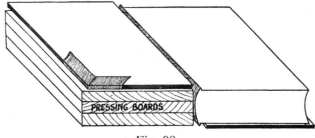

PRESSING BOARDS

Fig. 98

of the board with the folder and then draw it over on to the board with the side of the hand.  Tuck in the corner with the point of the folder or thumb-nail and turn in the overlap on the fore-edge.  Tap the corner neatly into shape with the folder and set the mitre accurately.  Again tap the edges of the leather as square as may be, but avoid that sharp-edged squareness beloved by some binders as it is not in keeping with the nature of the material and is very liable to damage when the book is in use.  Attach all four corners in the same way.

ATTACHING THE LEATHER BACK.  31. For the purpose of strengthening the headcap have ready two pieces of thick string the length of which should be equal to the width across the spine of the book from groove to groove.  The "headcap" is the turned-over leather at the head and tail of the spine.

32. Repaste the leather for the back, working the paste well into the surface, remove all excess paste—there should be none left lying on the surface. Rub a little paste well into the back of the book and then lay the back exactly on the centre of the pasted leather. See that there is an equal overlap at the head and tail and also an equal amount of leather to overlap on to each side of the book. Press the back down on to the leather to make it stick and then pick up the leather with the book and wrap the overlap on to each board. See that this overlap is equal on each board and then lay the book on its side on the bench. Make sure that the leather adheres all over the back of the book by rolling the flat of the folder across the spine in order to press the leather firmly against the back of the book.

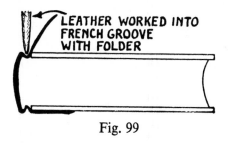

LEATHER WORKED INTO FRENCH GROOVE WITH FOLDER

Fig. 99

Lift the leather from the side of the board carefully and work it down into the French groove with a folder, fig. 99, and then lay the leather down on to the board again and work it firmly into place. If the rubbing down into the groove is done without first lifting the leather from the side it will become stretched across the joint and tend to pull the leather on the back and sides out of place. Turn the book over and repeat for the other side. Again work the leather against the back of the book to ensure that it adheres all over the spine. See plate X.

33. The head and tail overlaps have now to be turned in. Open both boards and place a scrap of waste paper on the pasted leather at the tail, to prevent it from soiling the leaves and stand the book upright on the bench, fig. 100. Place one of the prepared pieces of string on the leather level with the head of the book. Rub a little paste on the outside of the leather at the turn-in. With one hand on the top edge of each board push back the boards slightly

and fold over the leather with the thumbs so that the string is kept in place, level with the top of the book. Smooth out any creases that may have formed and see that the turn-in over the string is quite flat to prevent any ridge showing on the spine of the book. Check the position of

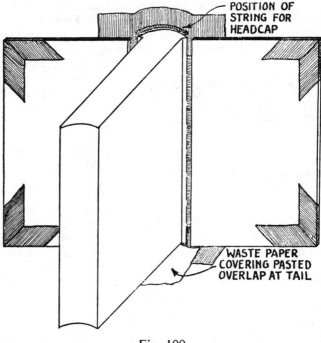

POSITION OF
STRING FOR
HEADCAP

WASTE PAPER
COVERING PASTED
OVERLAP AT TAIL

Fig. 100

the string to make quite certain that it has not slipped—which it very frequently does. If necessary, open up the turn-in and try again. Repeat for the tail in the same way and tap up the leather along the edge of the board so that it is reasonably square.

**SETTING THE HEADCAPS.** 34. Tie a piece of string firmly round the book so that it lies along the French groove, fig. 101. Note the position of the knot—between the boards at the head or tail. If the knot lies at the side on the damp leather it will leave a dent in the surface. Insert the point

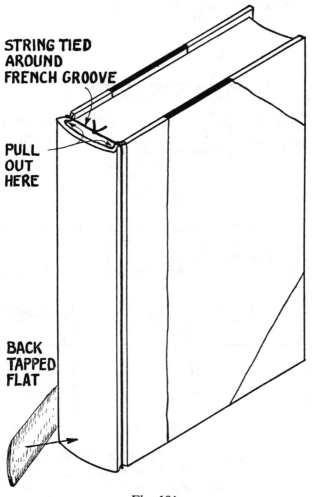

STRING TIED
AROUND
FRENCH GROOVE

PULL
OUT
HERE

BACK
TAPPED
FLAT

Fig. 101

of the folder between the string and the headcap and pull out the corners of the headcap carefully to give it a good shape, as indicated in fig. 101. Stand the book on its head on the bench and tap round the spine with the flat of the folder in order to work the headcap into position and to flatten the back, fig. 101.

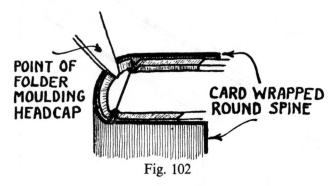

POINT OF
FOLDER
MOULDING
HEADCAP

CARD WRAPPED
ROUND SPINE

Fig. 102

35. Wrap a strip of thin card round the back of the book behind the headcap, this is to prevent the leather from being stretched away from the back of the book. Hold the card firmly in place with the left hand and mould the headcap

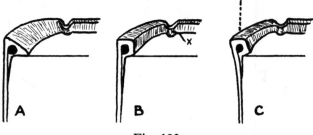

Fig. 103

to a pleasant shape with the point of the folder as shown in fig. 102. The headcap may be bevelled as in fig. 103A, or worked to a square section as shown at B. Care must be taken not to pull the headcap away from the spine of the book as shown at C, if this does occur the back must be tapped flat again as shown in fig. 101. The top of the headcap should not project above the level of the boards, particularly at the tail where it would be badly knocked about whilst being stood on the shelf when in use. Some binders leave the tail headcap slightly below the level of the boards for this reason.

36. Inspect the book to see that all is in order, since it will be impossible to make any adjustments once the leather has dried out. Take particular care to see that the back is quite flat and that the leather is adhering to it firmly all over the spine. Open the boards slightly and work out with the point of the folder any creases that may be found in the turn-in of the leather at the head and tail.

37. Place a waterproof sheet under each board to prevent the dampness of the leather from striking back and cockling or staining the endpaper. Place a sheet of clean paper round the outside and place the book between pressing boards which are set level with the grooves, and leave under a light weight to dry out—overnight at least. Do *not* press the book, otherwise the leather will be forced off the spine.

38. When the leather is dry, cut the string and open the book carefully. If the headcap tends to be a little too hard and tight for the boards to open easily, slightly damp the inside of the turn-in of the leather at the joint X, in fig. 103B, and allow it to stand for a short while. The leather should then have softened sufficiently for the boards to be opened freely.

TRIMMING THE LEATHER. 39. The edges of the leather will probably be a little uneven and will need marking-out in order to give the exact size of the cloth sides required. Measure from the fore-edge of the boards and make both sides of the book the same, S in fig. 104. Rule a line down each side with a folder, making a fairly bold groove, fig. 105A. Make all four corners equal in size by measuring with the dividers the distance from the corner of the board to the edge of the leather on the smallest corner. Mark all four corners with small ticks of the dividers to this distance,

C in fig. 104, and rule a line with the folder across each, again making a bold groove. The cloth side can now be put on up to these marks and so cover the unevenness of the edge of the leather. But this unevenness of the edge will show as a slight ridge under the side and a far neater job results if the waste is first trimmed away with a sharp knife. Hold the knife at a steep slant and cut just through the leather on the waste side of the folder line, as shown in fig. 105A. This

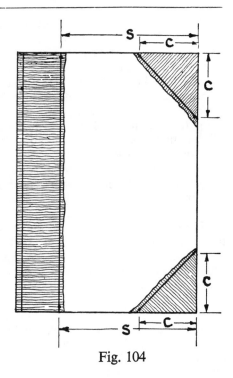

Fig. 104

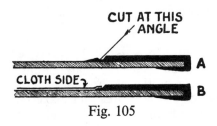

Fig. 105

cutting should be done without the assistance of a straight-edge in order to get the very steeply sloped cut needed. Peel away the waste leather on the surface of the board only, do *not* trim round the edge or on to the inside of the board.

SIDING. 40. Cut the cloth sides exactly as described for the sides of the single-sectioned binding on page 43. Paste them out and place them in position. They should just overlap the edge of the trimmed leather and the edge of the cloth should lie along the groove formed by the folder line as shown in fig. 105B.

**TRIMMING-OUT INSIDE.** 41. Trim out any unevenness of the overlap on the inside of the boards by marking round with

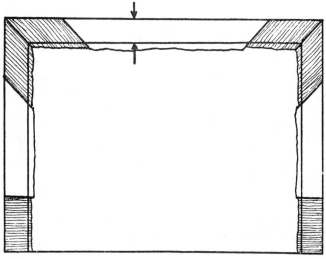

Fig. 106

the dividers and then trimming out with a sharp knife, fig. 106.

**PASTING-DOWN SHUT.** 42. Paste the endpapers and shut down the boards on to them. Nip in the press. Inspect carefully and then allow the book to dry out under a light weight.

## Chapter X

# BINDING SINGLE SHEETS

THE binding of single sheets of written or typed work is quite often required and the following method is suggested as a simple and effective way of dealing with the problem. It presupposes that there is a plain margin down the left-hand side of the sheets. This margin should be $1\frac{1}{4}''$ wide, the very minimum being about $1''$, if less than this the written material at the edge of the pages cannot be read as it gets bound up in the joint at the back. If the margin is too small the alternative method given at the end of this chapter can be used although it is a slightly more difficult method of binding.

Style:—Stab-sewn, turned in all round. Cloth back with paper sides.

1. Cut two single endpapers the same size as the sheets and place one at each end of the pile of sheets.

2. Cut two boards with one corner square. Make them about $\frac{1}{2}''$ longer and wider than the sheets.

3. Knock up the sheets between the boards so that the back and the head are square. If the words are so near the front edge that it must be left uncut, it will be found better to knock up to the *front* edge so as to make it as flat as possible.

GLUING-UP THE BACK. 4. Place the book in the lying press with about $1''$ of the back of the book projecting, fig. 107. Make sure that the back of the book is quite flat, then glue the back. Work the glue well in between the sheets with a dabbing motion of the brush.

5. Take the book from the press, remove the boards and place the book on one side for the glue to set.

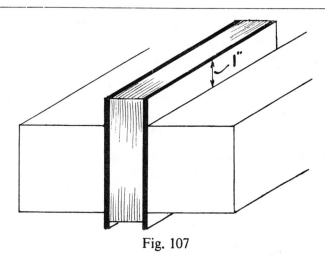

Fig. 107

**CUTTING THE BOARDS TO SIZE.**     6. Trim away the glued edge of the boards, cutting them to the same width as the sheets and with the head square with the back edge. Next cut off a strip $\frac{5}{8}''$ wide from the back edge of each board,

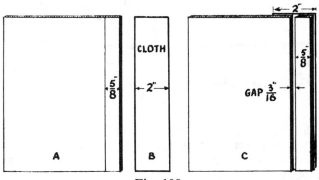

Fig. 108

fig. 108A. If the margin is very narrow this strip could be reduced to $\frac{1}{2}''$.

7. Cut two strips of cloth 2″ wide and of the same length as the boards, fig. 108B.

**PREPARING THE HINGED BOARDS.** 8. Paste the reverse side of the cloth strip and place one of the $\frac{5}{8}''$ strips of board on the cloth level with one edge and the other part of the board over the rest of the cloth. Leave a space, equal to a little more than twice the thickness of the boards, between the strip and the main board; about $\frac{3}{16}''$ will be found about right for 1-lb. boards, fig. 108C. Press the boards well down on to the cloth and give them a quick nip.

**ATTACHING THE BOARDS TO THE BOOK.** 9. Turn the boards over so that the cloth hinge is uppermost. Place a guard of waste paper or card on top so that $\frac{1}{2}''$ of the back edge of the cloth is exposed, fig. 109A. Glue this exposed strip of

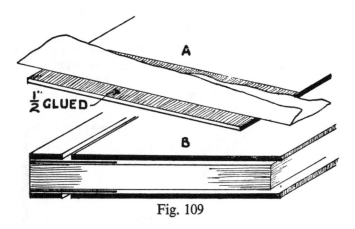

Fig. 109

cloth. Place the board accurately on the book so that the $\frac{5}{8}''$ strip lies exactly along the back edge of the book and the head level. The cloth hinge lies on the inside next to the book, fig. 109B.

**STAB-SEWING THE BOOK.** 10. Mark the position of three holes in the middle of the $\frac{5}{8}''$ strip. One $\frac{1}{2}''$ from each end of the book and the third in the centre. Divide the remaining distance between them into equal spaces of not more than $1\frac{1}{2}''$ and stab holes at these points with a fine awl. All the stab holes should go right through the thickness of the book to enable the sewing to be done more easily, fig. 110A.

11. Sew through the holes with a double thread in exactly the same manner as described for single section sewing,

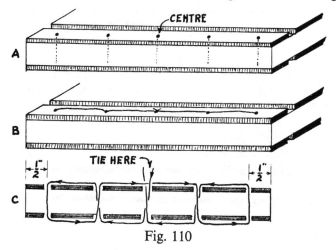

Fig. 110

fig. 110C. Start and finish at the centre hole and then tie a knot across the long centre stitch and cut off the excess thread leaving tails of about $\frac{3}{8}''$.

12. Place the book flat on the bench and gently hammer along the strip so that the knot and the thread become slightly embedded in the board.

COVERING THE BACK WITH CLOTH. 13. Cut a strip of cloth the same length as the boards. The width must be sufficient to cover the back and to overlap on to each side for 2'', i.e., the width of the cloth is 4'' plus the thickness of the book, fig. 111.

14. Mark the cloth on the reverse side with two lines down the centre, their distance apart being equal to the thickness of the book, fig. 111.

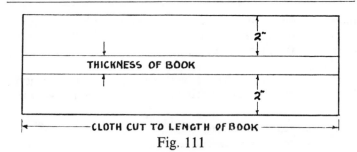

Fig. 111

15. Paste the reverse side of the cloth. Place the back of the book exactly to the pencil lines. Lift the cloth and rub it well down on to the back of the book and over on to

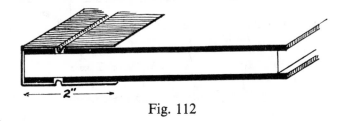

Fig. 112

the $\frac{5}{8}''$ strips of board. Then rub the cloth into the hinge with the folder and lay the rest of the cloth down on to the sides, fig. 112. Allow the paste to dry.

**MARKING AND CUTTING THE EDGES.** 16. Make two marks on the sides of the book at equal distances from the back. The distance should exactly equal the width of the pages of the book, fig. 113.

17. Place a piece of waste card at the front just below the two marks and parallel with them and another piece of card at the back as a cut-against. Lower the book into the cutting press until the front card is exactly level with the cheek of the press. Screw the press up tightly keeping the cheeks parallel. Check to see that the back of the book is quite flat in the press, fig. 114.

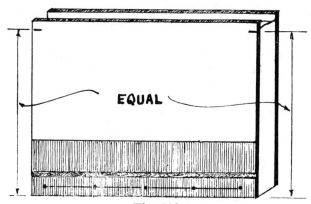

Fig. 113

18. Sharpen the plough blade and plough off the waste.

19. Using a try-square or the square corner of a piece of card, square a line across at the head and tail of the book and plough off the waste with the back of the book placed nearest to the worker.  The book is now "cut-flush".

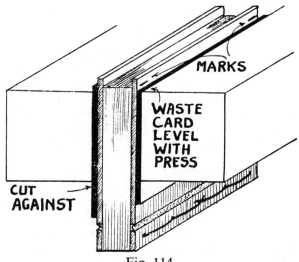

Fig. 114

**SIDING THE BOOK.** 20. If quarter-bound the paper sides are put on next. They should overlap the edges of the cloth back by $\frac{1}{8}''$ and be turned in over the edges of the boards for $\frac{5}{8}''$, fig. 115A. If half-binding is preferred the cloth corners are put on first and then the paper sides, as described on page 43 for the single-sectioned book.

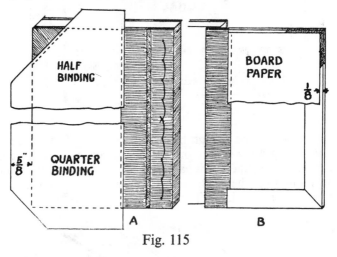

Fig. 115

**LINING THE BOARDS.** 21. Cut a sheet of paper to match the endpaper. The size should be such that when it lies on the inside of the board it is $\frac{1}{8}''$ away from the edge at the head, tail and fore-edge and just overlaps the edge of the cloth hinge by $\frac{1}{8}''$, fig. 115B. Paste this "board paper" and lay it in position. Repeat for the other end and then nip in the press. Leave under a light weight to dry out.

### ALTERNATIVE METHOD
### OF BINDING SINGLE SHEETS

Useful when the words are so near the left-hand edge of the page that sheets cannot be stab-sewn.

1. Knock-up the sheets square between boards and glue the back and allow the glue to set, as described in paragraphs 2 to 5 above.

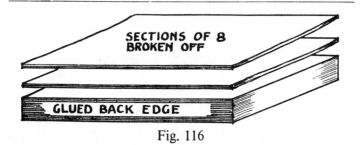

Fig. 116

2. Break off the sheets, in groups of about 8, from the glued pile. These will now form the sections of the book, fig. 116.

**OVER-SEWING OR WHIP-STITCHING.** 3. Over-sew the glued back edge of each section with a single thread of silk for $\frac{1}{8}''$, starting and finishing $\frac{3}{8}''$ from each end with a double stitch. The stitches should be about $\frac{1}{2}''$ apart, fig. 117.

4. Very gently hammer the stitches along the back edge of each section.

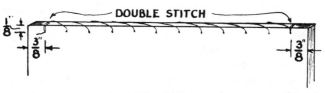

Fig. 117

5. Treat these over-sewn sections exactly as the ordinary sections of a multi-sectioned book and bind in case, hollow-back, or library style, as desired. Avoid sawing-in the kettle-stitch owing to the danger of cutting the whip-stitching. A book of this type is difficult to "back" and it is best left with a flat back or just rounded slightly.

# Chapter XI

## LETTERING A BOOK

**WRITTEN LABELS.** The simplest method of titling a book is to use a paper label on which the title has been written with lettering pens and Indian ink. The label is pasted or thin glued and placed on the side or spine of the book. It is more convenient for writing the title if the piece of paper is large enough to handle comfortably, the title-piece being afterwards cut out to the required size, fig. 118.

Fig. 118

A neat appearance is given to the paper label on the side of the book if it is stuck down into a slight depression formed in the cover. This is also functional in that it lowers the paper below the surface of the book and so protects the edges of the label from being rubbed up.

The depression must be made soon after the side of the book has been covered and while the surface is still slightly damp. Cut a piece of card to the size of the required depression, place it carefully in position on the side of the book and then place the book in the press between pressing boards. Great care is necessary to prevent the small piece of card from moving before it is pressed—a small spot of paste in the centre of the card helps to keep it in place—any mark left will be covered by the label. Make certain that the small piece of card is exactly under the centre of the screw of the press so as to produce a depression of even depth, then screw down the press tightly for a few minutes. If the label is made $\frac{1}{16}''$ shorter and narrower than the

*PLATE X*

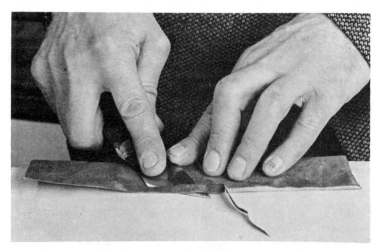

PARING LEATHER WITH AN EDGING KNIFE (*v. Page* 102)

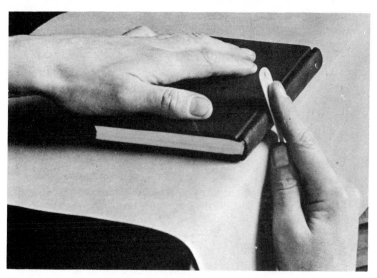

ENSURING THAT THE LEATHER ADHERES TO THE SPINE OF THE BOOK
BY PRESSING WITH A FOLDER OR FLAT STICK (*v. Page* 105)

*PLATE XI*

METHOD OF USING THE HAND
TOOLS (*v. Page* 121)

RETOUCHING A FAULTY
IMPRESSION (*v. Page* 127)

TOOLING THE SPINE OF A BOOK (*v. Page* 126)

depression it will fit in neatly leaving a slight border all round the edge.

**TOOLED LABELS.** For the first practice with the hand-tool letters, labels can be made with the aid of an ordinary inking pad, fig. 119. Press the cold tool on to the pad to pick up the ink and then press it on to the paper label, allow the ink to dry—it usually takes some time—and then paste the label in position as described for the written labels. As an assistance in positioning the letters correctly they can first be very lightly pressed on the paper without inking so that a light "blind" impression is produced. This can be adjusted, if necessary, and when the position is correct the tool can be inked and replaced in the blind impression.

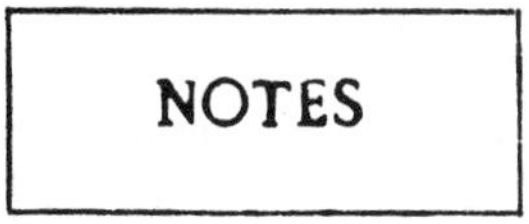

```
┌─────────────────────────┐
│                         │
│        NOTES            │
│                         │
└─────────────────────────┘
```

Fig. 119

**USING THE HAND TOOLS.** Much practice will be needed before the tools can be impressed accurately so that the letters are all perfectly vertical and in alignment as well as evenly spaced.

First, rule a fine pencil line on the paper—the letters will be placed *below* this line and not above it. Grip the handle of the tool in the palm of the right hand, with the thumb on top of the handle. Dab the face of the tool on the inking pad—check to see that the letter is the right way up, i.e., that the file mark across the shank of the tool is to the top, indicating the top of the letter. Guide the tool with the point of the left thumb and press the tool lightly on to the paper. Without moving the position of the tool rock the handle very slightly forwards and backwards and also from side to side to ensure an even impression. See plate XI.

The pressure used on the tool is quite light—the old craftsmen say, "Just twice the weight of the tool,"—this "touch" can only be obtained by experiment and experience. Too much pressure is the commonest fault, particularly on the narrower letters like "I" and also on the comma, full stop, etc. These can quite easily be pressed right through the material unless great care is taken.

When sighting the position of the tool in relation to the pencil line on the paper it will be found that more accurate alignment can be obtained if the letter is placed slightly *below* the line, i.e., leaving just a "hair-space" between the line and the top of the letter, see fig. 120.

Fig. 120

The spacing of the letters requires nice judgment since the letters themselves vary in width, e.g., the M and the I, and this has to be allowed for or the result may look a little odd. If we consider the widths of the various letters, the letter H can be taken as of average width as compared with the wide O, M and W, etc., and the narrow I, E, B, S, etc.

Take a letter H and make a few impressions side by side in line so that they are pleasantly spaced, being neither too close together nor too far apart, fig. 120. When the spacing is satisfactory set a pair of dividers to the distance between the centre of one letter and the centre of the next.

Write out the required title on a piece of scrap paper and count the number of letters, counting the space between words as one letter, e.g., THE BLACK TULIP would be counted as 15 letters. Find also the centre of the line, i.e., in

THE BLACK TULIP

Fig. 121

this case the middle letter is C, fig. 121.

Rule a fine pencil line on the paper to give the position of the first line of lettering. Mark also the centre by means of a vertical line or by folding the paper in half at right-angles to the ruled line. Now make ticks with the dividers on the *top* side of the line, starting at the centre and working outwards on each side, see figs. 124 and 125. This gives a rough preliminary spacing for the letters of the title, but adjustment will have to be made as the letters are tooled, to allow for their varying widths. The tooling is started at the centre and worked outwards on each side making any necessary adjustments as the work proceeds.

When the lettering has to be in more than one line the distance between the bottom of the letters on the first line and the top of the letters in the next should be rather less than the height of the letters. If the lettering is in a panel on the spine of a book, the space below the bottom line of letters should be rather greater than the space above the top line. See fig. 126.

Plenty of practice will be required before any real skill can be developed in tooling.

**LETTERING WITH PRINTER'S INK.** Lettering can be done with printer's ink by first pressing the tool on to a smooth surface upon which a little ink has been rolled out thinly by means of a small roller. Blind tooling the impression first enables the setting out to be adjusted, if necessary, before the permanent ink is applied.

**LETTERING WITH THE HEATED TOOLS AND CARBON PAPER.** The first introduction to the use of heated tools is best done by the use of carbon paper. If the warm tool is dabbed on to a sheet of carbon paper the heat will melt the ink

Fig. 122

which will be picked up on the face of the tool. If the tool is then applied to the material a clear, dark impression is obtained.

**HEATING THE TOOLS FOR LETTERING.** Lay out the tools on the finishing stove in the order in which they will be required and let them warm up gently. Keep the wooden handles well away from the heat as they very easily get burnt and thus rendered useless.

To test the heat of the tool, place the side of the shank on to a piece of wet rag or cotton-wool which is standing in a saucer, fig. 122. The tool should be removed from the cooler just before it ceases to hiss—the hiss should not be killed completely or the tool will be too cool—except for use with the carbon paper when the tool can be much cooler. Quickly rub the face of the tool on the flesh side of a leather pad so that the face is quite clean and then impress the tool where required.

In cooling the tool make quite certain that it is not too hot or it will very easily burn right through the material! Note that it is the *side* of the shank that is cooled and not the end. If the end were cooled the shank might still retain too much heat and this would then run back to the point and make it too hot again.

**LETTERING WITH GOLD FILM OR GOLD FOIL.** Film or foil as its name implies consists of thin sheets coated with gold or gold substitute and a special preparation such that, when the sheet is laid on to paper, cloth or leather and the heated tool impressed through it, the gold is transferred to the material in the impression of the tool.

To enable the tooling to be done accurately the title should first be set out by means of the cold tool and inking pad. This is done on thin *bank* paper—avoid thick paper as this would later insulate the heat of the tool and so cause poor impressions. The foil is then cut a little larger than the area of lettering and placed on the reverse side of the paper. Great care should be taken to see that the foil is placed the correct way round to the paper, otherwise it may be found when the tooling is completed, that all the gold is adhering to the back of the bank paper and that there is none on the book. One side of the foil is yellowish in colour and the other golden, it is this golden side that should be next to the bank paper so that when tooled this face will be uppermost on the book. An experiment with a hot tool and a scrap of foil will soon remove any doubt.

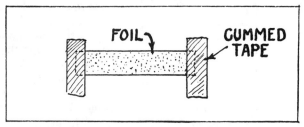

Fig. 123

The foil should be held in place on the reverse side of the paper by means of small pieces of gummed tape or by very small spots of paste, fig. 123. Make certain that the foil completely covers the area of the lettering—holding the paper up to the light will show clearly whether the foil is correctly placed or not. Take care that the gummed tape or the paste does not come directly behind any of the letters or else the tooling of those particular letters will be ineffective.

The bank paper must now be attached to the book in the correct position in order that the lettering can be tooled through with the heated tools and thus transfer the title in gold to the surface of the book.

TOOLING ON THE SPINE. The paper should be about 3″ deep and long enough to lap on to the sides of the book for about 1½″, fig. 124.

Place the book in the finishing press with a sheet of card up to the groove on each side. The back of the book should be sloping so that the head is slightly higher than the tail, this enables the tooling to be done in a more comfortable position. Make sure that the book is the *right way round*—it is so very easy to put the title on upside down!

Find the centre of the spine by measuring from each side with the dividers and make a faint pencil line down the

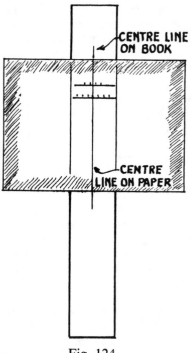

Fig. 124

centre of the spine. Place the paper on the spine with the title in the required position towards the head of the book. Carefully adjust the centre line on the paper so that it exactly coincides with the faint pencil line down the centre of the spine, fig. 124. Fix the paper firmly in place, by means of strips of gummed tape or spots of paste, on to the cards at the sides. Check to see that the title is exactly central and that the lettering is square across the spine of the book. See plate XI. It is then ready for tooling.

Heat up the tools and, after cooling them on the wet pad so that they are still just sizzling gently, impress them accurately on the letters on the paper, rocking the tool very slightly so as to produce an even impression. This process needs great care to ensure good results.

When the tooling is completed, release the paper at one side only and, while still holding it in place, lift one side until the result of the tooling is visible. If any letters have been missed or require a further touch with the tool, replace the paper carefully and re-tool where necessary.

This care in inspecting the tooling is very necessary since if the paper is removed completely, it is next to impossible to replace it accurately in exactly the right spot for the purpose of retouching.

Should any retouching be required after the paper has been removed, correct registration of the letter when re-tooling can be ensured if the edge of a piece of foil is placed on the faulty letter covering only the untooled portion. The tooled part of the letter which is left exposed will enable the hot tool to be replaced exactly on the letter and so correct any faulty impression on the other part. See plate XI.

A rub with a piece of clean rag will remove any bits of gold blurring the edges of the impressions.

**TOOLING ON THE SIDE.** Letter out the title on a piece of thin bank paper as before and fix the foil behind it. Check to see that the *front* of the book is being dealt with

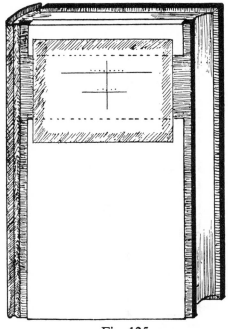

Fig. 125

and that the head is uppermost! Place a sheet of waste paper under the front cover and wrap the ends round on to the front at the head and tail. The paper should be just a fraction narrower than the board of the book. Place the title in the required position on the side of the book and fix it to the waste flaps at the head and tail by means of dabs of paste or gummed tape, fig. 125. Make sure that the title-piece is firmly fixed and that it is not liable to move during the progress of the tooling. Tool with heated tools as described above.

The position of the title is usually towards the top of the book where it looks best. Accurate alignment can be aided by testing the lines of letters by means of a try-square placed against the fore-edge of the cover board.

**BLIND TOOLING ON LEATHER.** Blind tooling is the making of impressions with the tool but without gold or colour. It is particularly effective on leather of a light colour since the impressions can be made dark by the heat of the tool so that they stand out quite clearly.

Make out the title on paper as before and tool quite lightly through it on to the leather with warm tools.

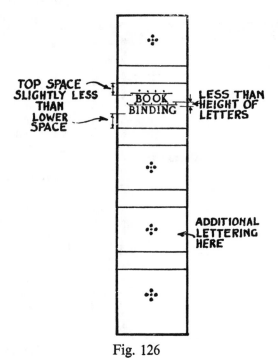

Fig. 126

Remove the paper and make any necessary adjustments in the position of the letters. Next damp the leather all over and re-tool the letters—the tools should be heated and then cooled on the pad so that the sizzle is just killed. Beware of using the tool too hot on the damp leather or burnt impressions can easily result. The heat of the tool will darken the leather in the impression. Every effort must be made to make the darkening as even as possible over all the letters.

**TOOLING THE SPINES OF LIBRARY STYLE BOOKS.** Books bound in library style—with the leather stuck directly to the spine of the book—inevitably show slight bumps due to the tapes. The appearance of the back of the book is greatly improved if the position of the tapes is emphasised

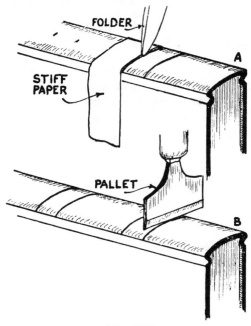

Fig. 127

by tooling with blind lines across the spine. This practically conceals the unevenness that was so apparent before tooling, fig. 126.

Step off with the dividers the position of the tapes on the spine, so that the lines can be accurately spaced, and mark their position by small ticks, fig. 127A. Fold a piece of stiff paper to form a straight-edge and wrap it round the spine of the book so that its edge is quite horizontal. Use it as a guide for marking-in all the lines with the point of a folder. Make sure that the lines are all horizontal and parallel with one another. Tool them in with a line pallet, after first damping the spine all over, to produce the darkened blind line, fig. 127B. "Jiggering" the pallet, i.e., rubbing it backwards and forwards in the line, produces a polish in the blind tooling.

The title, which can be blind or in gold, is always placed in the second space from the top, any further lettering that may be required is placed in the fourth space. The remaining blank spaces are very effectively—and sufficiently—decorated by impressing a very simple tool in the centre of each space, fig. 126. Nothing more elaborate in the way of decoration is required or even desirable on books of this type which are intended to stand up to hard wear.

# Appendix

# SEQUENCE OF OPERATIONS

IT has been found that although the individual operations in bookbinding are not very difficult to learn there are such a number of them that students frequently omit some, or try to do them in the wrong order. To overcome this difficulty it is helpful to work from a list of the operations similar to that shown below. The number at the end of each line indicates the page on which a detailed account of the operation can be found.

## SINGLE SECTION BINDING

**HALF CLOTH.**
1. Choose cloth and paper for cover and endpapers, 33.
2. Prepare endpapers, 33.
3. Remove old sewing thread or metal clips from book, 34.
4. Stick linen strip outside the endpapers, 34.
5. Mark up and sew the book through the linen strip, 34.
6. Cut edges of book, 36.
7. Cut boards to size; $\frac{1}{4}''$ longer and $\frac{1}{8}''$ narrower than book, 22, 38.
8. Attach boards to book, 38.
9. Nip book in press—waste sheet under boards, 30.
10. Cut cloth for back and corners from paper patterns, 39.
11. Attach cloth corners, 40.
12. Attach cloth back, 41.
13. Nip book in press—waste sheet under boards, 30.
14. Prepare paper sides, 43.
15. Attach paper sides, 44.
16. Nip book in press—waste sheet under boards, 30.
17. Paste down the endpapers, 44.
18. Nip the book in the press, 30.
19. Allow book to dry under light pressure, 45.

## CASE BINDING

**FULL CLOTH.**

1. Choose endpapers and cloth for cover, 33.
2. Prepare sections for rebinding, 47.
3. Cut boards to rough size—one corner square, 54.
4. Knock up sections and mark up for sewing, 54.
5. Saw-in kettle-stitch marks, 56.
6. Collate, 53.
7. Sew book on tapes, 56.
8. Knock down the swelling if necessary, 60.
9. Paste up first and last sections, $\frac{1}{8}''$ only, 61.
10. Tip on endpapers with paste, $\frac{1}{8}''$ only, 62.
11. Glue back square and flat, tapes *inside*, 63.
12. When nearly dry cut fore-edge, 64.
13. Round the back, 67.
14. Back the book, tapes *outside*, 68.
15. Glue mull to back of book, 70.
16. Line up the back with paper, 71.
17. Cut the boards to final size, 71.
18. Cut the head and tail of the book, 72, 74.
19. Make the case, 75.
20. Stick down tapes and mull to endpaper, 74.
21. Paste down the book into the case, 76.
22. Nip the book in the press, 77.
23. Allow book to dry under light pressure, 77.

## HOLLOW BACKED BINDING

QUARTER CLOTH.
1. Choose cloth and paper for cover and endpapers, 33.
2. Prepare endpapers, 81.
3. Prepare sections for rebinding, 47.
4. Cut boards to rough size, one corner square, 54.
5. Knock up square between boards, *omitting* endpapers, 54.
6. Mark up for sewing on tapes, 54.
7. Saw-in kettle-stitch marks, 56.
8. Replace endpapers and mark for sewing, 88.
9. Collate, 53.
10. Sew the book including the endpapers, 56.
11. Knock down the swelling, 60.
12. Paste up first and last sections and endpapers, 61.
13. Glue the back square and flat, tapes *inside*, 63.
14. When nearly dry, cut fore-edge, 64.
15. Round the back, 67.
16. Back the book, tapes *outside*, 68.
17. Line-up the back with mull, 70.
18. Cut boards to finished size, 89.
19. Cut the head and tail of the book, 72, 74.
20. Stick down tapes and mull to waste sheet, 74.
21. Attach boards to book, 89.
22. Attach hollow back, 89.
23. Slit hollow and hinge for 1″, 90.
24. Cut cloth for back from paper pattern, 91.
25. Cover back of book with cloth, 92.
26. Cut paper for sides, 93.
27. Cover sides with paper, 94.
28. Nip the book in the press, 77.
29. Paste down the endpapers, 94.
30. Nip the book in the press, 77.
31. Allow the book to dry out under light pressure, 95.

## LIBRARY STYLE

**HALF LEATHER.**

1. Choose leather and cloth for cover and endpapers, 33.
2. Make a pair of split boards, 96.
3. Prepare endpapers, 81.
4. Prepare sections for rebinding, 47.
5. Cut spare boards to rough size—one corner square, 54.
6. Knock up square between boards, *omitting* endpapers, 54.
7. Mark up for sewing on at least four tapes, 54.
8. Saw-in kettle-stitch marks, 56.
9. Replace endpapers and mark for sewing, 97.
10. Collate, 53.
11. Sew the book and endpapers, 56.
12. Knock down the swelling, 60, 97.
13. Paste up first and last sections and endpapers, 61, 97.
14. Glue the back square and flat, tapes *inside*, 63.
15. When nearly dry cut the fore-edge, 64.
16. Round the back, 67.
17. Back the book, tapes *outside*, 68.
18. Line up the back with mull, 70.
19. Cut the split boards to final size, 97.
20. Cut the head and tail of the book, 72, 74.
21. Trim boards to make allowance for groove, 98.
22. Stick tapes and mull to waste sheet, 99.
23. Trim off slips $1\frac{1}{4}''$ wide, 99.
24. Attach split boards to book, 100.
25. Press with tins inside, 100.
25. Cut leather back and corners from paper patterns, 101.
26. Pare leather back and corners, 101.
27. Paste and attach leather corners, 103.
28. Paste and attach leather back, 104.
29. Tie up and set headcaps, 106.
30. Place waterproof sheets under boards, 109.
31. Allow to dry under light weight, twenty-four hours, 109.
32. Open up the book carefully, 109.
33. Trim the leather on the *outside* only, 109.

34. Cut cloth (or paper) sides, 44, 110.
35. Attach sides and nip in press, 77.
36. Trim out inside of covers, 111.
37. Paste down the endpapers, 94.
38. Nip in the press, 77.
39. Allow the book to dry out under light pressure, 111.

## BINDING SINGLE SHEETS

**STAB-SEWN, TURNED IN ALL ROUND.**
1. Choose cloth, paper sides and endpapers, 33.
2. Cut endpapers to size of sheets, 112.
3. Cut boards to rough size—one corner square, 112.
4. Knock up square between boards, 112.
5. Glue the back edge of the sheets, 112.
6. Remove boards and allow glue to dry, 112.
7. Cut boards to same size as sheets, 113.
8. Cut off strip ⅛" wide from one edge, 113.
9. Cut piece of cloth 2" wide for hinge, 113.
10. Attach strip and rest of board to cloth, 114.
11. Attach boards to book, 114.
12. Stab-sew the book through strip, 114.
13. Tap stitches flat with hammer, 115.
14. Cut cloth for back, 115.
15. Cover back of book with cloth, 116.
16. Nip in the press, 77.
17. Allow the book to dry thoroughly.
18. Cut the fore-edge, head and tail, 117.
19. Cut paper sides to size, 118.
20. Attach sides to book, 118.
21. Nip the book in the press, 77.
22. Cut board-paper to match endpaper, 118.
23. Paste down the board-paper, 118.
24. Nip the book in the press, 77.
25. Allow the book to dry under a light pressure, 111.

# SUPPLIERS OF
# BOOKBINDING MATERIALS

*(Many of the sources listed have catalogues and samples available.)*

Arcon Coating Mills
3067 New Street
Oceanside, NY 11572
　Binding tapes (for reinforcement
　of spine or first and last signa-
　tures); end sheets

Basic Crafts Co.
1201 Broadway
New York, NY 10001
　Bookbinding tools and supplies;
　gold-stamping type, holders,
　foils and stamps; leathers and
　cloths; end papers; how-to
　books; marbling supplies, kit
　and how-to books

Dick Blick
P.O. Box 1267
Galesburg, IL 61401
　Table cutter for cardboard and
　leather

The Davey Company
164 Laidlaw Avenue
P.O. Box 8128
Five Corners Station
Jersey City, NJ 07306
　Binder's board

Demco Inc.
P.O. Box 7488
Madison, WI 53707
　or
P.O. Box 7767
Fresno, CA 93747
　General bookbinding supplies;
　manual and videotape on book
　preservation and repair; various
　book repair kits

Gane Brothers and Lane Inc.
1400 Greenleaf Avenue
Elk Grove Village, IL 60007
　also
Maryland Heights, MO; Dallas,
TX; Atlanta, GA; Vernon, CA;
Conshohocken, PA
　General bookbinding supplies
　and equipment

Gaylord Brothers
P.O. Box 710
Stockton, CA 95201
　or
P.O. Box 4901
Syracuse, NY 13221
　Book mending supplies; manual
　on book-repair, *Bookcraft*

Guide of Book Workers Inc.
521 Fifth Avenue
New York, NY 10175
    Members receive a supplier directory and news about bookbinding

Hickok Bookbinders Equipment
W. O. Hickok Manufacturing
Ninth and Cumberland Streets
Harrisburg, PA 17103
    Large presses, cutters and other heavy equipment for binderies

MacPherson Leather
519 12th Avenue South
Seattle, WA 98144
    Leather and leather tools

McManus and Morgan Inc.
2506 West 7th Street
Los Angeles, CA 90057
    Fine papers; extensive line of bookbinding supplies

Montana Leather
2015 First Avenue North
Billings, MT 59103
    Leather and leather tools

Oregon Leather Company
110 N.W. 2nd Avenue
Portland, OR 97209
    Leather and leather tools

Ernest Schaeffer, Inc.
731 Lehigh Avenue
Union, NJ 07083
    General bookbinding supplies

Talas
Division of Technical Library
    Services
213 West 35th Street
New York, NY 10001
    General bookbinding supplies

The Tandy Leather Company
P.O. Box 791
Fort Worth, TX 76101
(184 stores throughout the country)
    Leather, leather tools; bone folders (nylon); linen thread; metal plates and rivets for telephone books covers

Zellerbach Paper Company
245 Spruce Avenue
San Francisco, CA 94080
    Chipboard, papers

# INDEX

Adhesives, 18
Adjustable plough blade, 5
Alum, 31
Art canvas, 15
  linen, 15
  paper, 12
  vellum, 15
Attaching boards, *Pl. VI*
  hollow-backed book, 89
  library style book, 100
  single-section book, 38
  stab-sewn book, 114
Attaching hollow back, 89
  leather back, 104
  leather corners, 103
  split boards, 100
Awl, 3, 4, 35

Back, cloth, 39, 91
  flat, 78
  gluing, 63
  hollow, 90
  leather, 104
  round, 79
  rounding, 67
  single-section cloth, 41
  tight, 96
Backing, 68
  boards, 5, 6; *Pl. IV*
  errors in, 70
Bank paper, 12, 124
Basic operations, 19
Basil, 16
Binding, case, 54, 132
  full, 54
  half, 33
  hollow backed, 88, 133
  library style, 96, 134
  quarter, 88
  single section, 33, 131
  single sheets, 112, 135
  style of, 33
Blade, adjustable plough, 5, 66

Blanks, brass, 8
Blind tooling, 128
Board cutter, 5, 6, 22
  paper, 87, 118
Boards, 12
  backing, 5, 6; *Pl. IV*
  cutting, 5, 6; *Pl. IV*
  cutting a pair of, 22
  cutting to size, 38, 71, 89, 97
  fibre, 13
  hinged, 114
  mill, 13
  oiled, 18
  pressing, 5, 8, 29; *Pl. V*
  split, 44, 96
  straw, 12
Bone folder, 1, 2, 19; *Pl. II*
Book cloth, 14
Bound books, 81
Bowline, 60
Brass rod, 7, 8
Brushes, 1, 2; *Pl. II*
  use of, 26
Buckram, cotton, 15
  linen, 15

Cake glue, 18, 31
Calf, 16
Canvas, art, 15
Cape morocco, 16
Carbon paper, lettering with, 123
Cardboard, see strawboard, 12
  knife, 1, 2; *Pl. II*
Card cutter, 5, 6, 22; *Pl. IV*
  cutting thick, 23
Cartridge paper, 11
Case binding, 54, 132
  binding, endpapers for, 62
  fixing book in, 76
  making, 75
Cased books, 54
Casing a book, 76
Catalogues, size of, 11

Cloth, 14
  back, 39, 91
  corners, 39
  cutting, 20
  full, 54
  half, 33
  jointed endpapers, 85
  quarter, 88
Cobbler's knife, 3, 4; *Pl. III*
Cockling of paper, 109
Cold-water paste, 18, 30
Collating, 53; *Pl. VIII*
Coloured paper, 11
Cooling pad, 123
Corners, cloth, 39
  leather, 103
  mitring, 40
  paring leather, 103
Cotton buckram, 15
Cover papers, 11
Covering hollow-backed book, 91
  library style book, 104
  single section book, 41
  stab sewn book, 115
Creases, 19
  removal of, 29
Crown, 10
Cut-against, 36
Cut flush, 117
Cutter, card, 5, 6 22; *Pl. IV*
Cutting, 20; *Pl. VI*
  boards, 5, 6; *Pl. IV*
  boards to size, 38, 72, 89, 97
  edge, safety, 1, 2
  fore-edge, 36, 64
  guards, 51
  head and tail, 37, 72
  pair of boards, 22
  thick card, 23

Demy, 10
Dividers, 2, 3; *Pl. II*
Double crown, 10
Dowel rod handles, 8
Drawing to the book, 83
Dutch strawboard, 12

Edge, safety cutting, 1, 2

Edging knife, 3, 4; *Pl. III*
Eightpenny, 14
Emery cloth, 3, 7
  paste, 3
Endpapers, 81
  cloth jointed, 85
  made, 46, 83
  pasting down, 44, 94
  pasting up, 88, 97
  patterned, 83
  sewing on, 88
  single section, 33, 45
  staining, 109
  tipping on, 62
  zig-zag, 81
English fibre board, 13
Equipment, 1; *Pls. II-V*
Exercise books, size, 10

Fence, setting, 22
Fibre board, 13
Film, gold, 124
Finishing off sewing, 60
  press, 125
  stove, 7, 8, 124; *Pl. V*
  tools, 5, 8
Flat back book, 78
  casing, 79
Flour paste, 31
Flush, cut, 117
Foil, attaching, 125
  gold, 124
Folder, 1, 2
  use of, 19; *Pl. X*
Folding, 19
Folio, 9, 10
Foolscap, 10
Fore-edge, cutting, 36, **64**
Forril, 16
Forwarding, 81
Frame, sewing, 3, 4, 56; *Pl. III*
French groove, 98
  paring knife, 3, 4; *Pl. III*
Full cloth binding, 54; *Pl. I*

Gas finishing stove, 7, 8; *Pl. V*
Glass for paring, 3

Glue, 18, 31
  pot, 3, 4; *Pl. III*
  preparation of, 31
Gluing up the back, 63
  single sheets, 112
Goat skin, 15
Gold film, 124
  foil, 124
Grain glue, 18, 31
Groove, French, 98
  knocking out old, 49
  making the, 68
Guarding plates, 52
  single sheets, 52
  torn sections, 51
Guards, cutting, 51
  paper for, 12
  pasting, 27

Half binding, 33; *Pl. I*
Hammer, 1, 2; *Pl. II*
Handles, tool, 8
Handling large sheets, 28
Handmade paper, 11
Hand tool letters, 5, 8
  using, 121; *Pl. XI*
Head, 34
  cutting the, 37, 72
Headcap, 104
  moulding the, 108
  setting the, 106
Heated tools, lettering with, 123
Hinged boards, 114
Hollow, 75
  making a, 90
Hollow-backed binding, 88, 133

Imitations, 9
Imperial, 10
India oilstone, 3
Ink, printer's, for lettering, 123
Iron, knocking down, 3, 4, 50, 60;
  *Pl. III*

Japanese vellum, 12
Jiggering, 130
Joining thread, 59

Joint, 70
  cloth, 85
  French, 98
  knocking out old, 49
Jointed endpapers, cloth, 85

Kettle stitch, 55, 59
  sawing-in, 56
Kitchen paper, 12
Knife, 1, 2
  cobbler's, 3, 4; *Pl. III*
  edging, 3, 4; *Pl. III*
  French paring, 3, 4; *Pl. III*
  plough, 24, 66
  sharpening, 23
Knocking-down iron, 3, 4, 50, 60;
  *Pl. III*
Knocking down the swelling, 60
  out old groove, 49
  up square, 54; *Pl. IX*
Knot, weaver's, 60

Labels, tooled, 121
  written, 120
Laminboard, 8; *Pl. V*
Large sheets, handling, 28
Leather, 15
  back, 101
  blind tooling, 128
  corners, 103
  paring, 101
  pasting, 103
Leaves, guarding loose, 52
Lettering a book, 120
  carbon paper, 123
  gold film, 124
  heated tools, 123
  Indian ink, 120
  printer's ink, 123
  retouching, 127
  setting out, 122
  spacing, 122
  tools, 5, 8; *Pl. V*
Levant morocco, 15
Library style binding, 96, 134
  tooling, 129
Line pallet, 130

Linen, art, 15
  buckram, 15
  tape, 17
  thread, 17
Lining back with mull, 34, 70
  back with paper, 71
  boards, 118
  strip, 75
  up cased books, 70
  up hollow back, 89
Linson, 11
Loose leaves, guarding, 52
Lying press, 5, 6; *Pl. IV*

Made endpapers, 46, 83
Manilla, 12
Marbled papers, 12
Marking-up for sewing, multi-
        sectioned book, 54
    single section book, 34
Materials, selection of, 9
Medium, 10
Mending sections, 51
  strips, paper for, 12
  strips, cutting, 51
Millboard, 13
  sizes of, 14
Mitres, setting, 104
Mitring corners, 40
Morocco, 15
Moulding headcaps, 108
Mull, 15
Mull, lining back with, 70
Multi-ply boards, 5, 8; *Pl. V*
Multi-sections, preparing, 47
Muslin, 15

Needles, 3
Newspapers for pasting, 12
  not for pressing, 29
Niger morocco, 15
Nipping, 30
  press, 5, 6, 29; *Pl. IV*
Novels, size of, 10

Oasis morocco, 15
Octavo, 9, 10

Oil, 3
Oiled boards, 18
Oilstone, 3, 4; *Pl. III*
  use of, 24
Open, pasting down, 94
Operations, basic, 19
  sequence of, 131
Overlaps, turning in, 28
Oversewing, 119

Pad, cooling, 123
Pallet, 7, 8, 130; *Pl. V*
  jiggering, 130
Paper, 9
  art, 12
  bank, 12, 124
  board, 87, 118
  cartridge, 11
  cockling of, 109
  coloured, 11
  cover, 11
  handmade, 11
  kitchen, 12
  lining up with, 71
  marbled, 12
  mending, 12
  pastel, 11
  patterned, 11
  waxed, 17
  weight of, 10
Parchment, 16
Paring, excessive, 17
  knives, 3, 4
  leather back, 102; *Pl. X*
  leather corners, 103
  stone, 3, 4; *Pl. III*
Paste, 18
  cold-water, 18, 30
  flour, 31
  preparation of, 30
Pastel paper, 11
Pasting, 26; *Pl. VII*
  guard, 27
  leather, 103
  newspapers for, 12
  up, 61, 88, 97
Pasting-down endpapers open, 94
    shut, 44, 94, 111

Patterned endpapers, 83
  papers, 11
  tools, 7, 8; *Pl. V*
Pearl glue, 18, 31
Pencil marks, 20
Persian leather, 16
Pigskin, 17
Plates, guarding, 52
Plough, 5, 6; *Pl. IV*
  blade, 5, 25
  cutting edges with, 36
  setting, 66
  sharpening blade of, 24
  using a, 67
Pocket, formation of, 28
Powder glue, 18, 32
Preparing for rebinding, 47
  glue, 31
  leather, 101
  paste, 30
  slips, 99
Press, finishing, 125
  lying, 5, 6; *Pl. IV*
  nipping, 5, 6, 29; *Pl. IV*
  standing, 5, 6, 29; *Pl. IV*
Pressing, 29
  boards, 5  8, 29; *Pl. V*
  book, 77
  sections, 50
Printer's ink, lettering, 123
Pulling, 47

Quarter binding, 88; *Pl. I*
  siding a, 93
Quarto, 9, 10
Quire, 9

Ream, 9
Rebinding, preparation for, 47
Repairing a section, 51
Retouching lettering, 127
Roan, 16
Rough calf, 16
Round back book, 79
Rounding back, 67
  errors in, 68
Royal, 10
Rubbing down, 29; *Pl. VI*

Russia leather, 16

Safety cutting edge, 1, 2
Saw, tenon, 1, 2; *Pl. II*
Sawing-in kettle stitch, 55
Scissors, 1
Scotch skin glue, 18, 31
Sealskin, 17
Section, binding single, 33, 131
Sections, mending torn, 51
  pasting up, 61, 88, 97
  pressing, 50
Selection of materials, 9
Sequence of operations, 131
Setting headcaps, 106
  mitres, 104
  out lettering, 122
  plough, 66
Sevenpenny, 14
Sewing endpapers, 88
  frame, 3, 4, 56; *Pl. III*
  finishing off, 60
  marking-up for, 54
  on tapes, 57
  single section, 34
  stab, 112
Sexto-decimo, 9, 10
Sharpening a knife, 23
  plough blade, 24
Sheepskins, 16
Sheets, binding single, 112, 118, 135
  guarding single, 52
  handling large, 28; *Pl. VII*
  sizes of paper, 9
Shut, pasting down, 94
Side, attaching, 44, 93
  preparing, 43
  tooling on, 127
Signatures, 48
Single section binding, 33, 131
Single sheets, binding, 112, 118, 135
  gluing up, 112
  guarding, 52
Sixpenny, 14
Sizes of millboard, 14
  paper, 10
  strawboard, 13

Skin glue, 18, 31
Skiver, 16
Slips, preparing, 99
Slitting, 19
  hollow back, 90
Spacing lettering, 122
Spine, tooling on, 125, 129
Split boards, 46, 96
  attaching, 100
Spring dividers, 2, 3; *Pl. II*
Square, 38
  try, 1, 2; *Pl. II*
Stab sewn, 112
Staining of endpaper, 109
Standard sizes of millboard, 14
  paper, 10
  strawboard, 13
Standing press, 5, 6, 29; *Pl. IV*
Starting, 68
Stitch, kettle, 55, 59
Stitching single section, 34
Stone, paring, 3, 4
Stove, finishing, 7, 8, 124; *Pl. V*
Straight-edge, for cutting, 1, 2, 20;
  *Pl. II*
Strawboard, 12
Stretching, 27
String for headcap, 104
Strop, 3, 4; *Pl. III*
Swelling, 60, 97
  knocking down the, 97

Tail, cutting, 37, 74
Tape, 17
  sewing on, 54, 57
Tenon saw, 1, 2; *Pl. II*
Tenpenny, 14
Text book, size of, 11
Thick card, cutting, 23
Thread, 17
  joining, 59
Three-ply boards, 8; *Pl. V.*
Tide-marks, 103
Tight back, 96
  pulling a, 48

Tipping, 27
  endpapers, 62
  single sheets, 52
Title, position of, 130
Tooled labels, 121
Tooling, blind, 128
  film or foil, 124
  library style, 128
  retouching, 127; *Pl. XI*
  sides, 127
  spine, 125, 129; *Pl. XI*
Tools, cooling, 123
  finishing, 5, 8
  hand, 121
  heated, 123
  letter, 5, 8; *Pl. V*
  pallet, 8; *Pl. V*
  patterned, 7, 8; *Pl. V*
Torn sections, mending, 51
Trimming, 20
  leather, 109
  out inside, 111
Try-square, 1, 2; *Pl. II*
Tub, 5, 6; *Pl. IV*
Turning in the overlaps, 28
Typed sheets, binding, 112
Tying up, 106

Vellum, 17
  art, 15
  Japanese, 12
Velvet calf, 16

Washita oilstone, 3
Waterproof sheets, 17, 18, 109
Waxed paper, 17
Weaver's knot, 60
Weight of paper, 10
Whipstitching, 119
Written labels, 120
  sheets, binding, 112

Zig-zag endpapers, 81

# A CATALOG OF SELECTED
# DOVER BOOKS
## IN ALL FIELDS OF INTEREST

# A CATALOG OF SELECTED DOVER
# BOOKS IN ALL FIELDS OF INTEREST

DRAWINGS OF REMBRANDT, edited by Seymour Slive. Updated Lippmann, Hofstede de Groot edition, with definitive scholarly apparatus. All portraits, biblical sketches, landscapes, nudes. Oriental figures, classical studies, together with selection of work by followers. 550 illustrations. Total of 630pp. 9⅛ × 12¼.
21485-0, 21486-9 Pa., Two-vol. set $29.90

GHOST AND HORROR STORIES OF AMBROSE BIERCE, Ambrose Bierce. 24 tales vividly imagined, strangely prophetic, and decades ahead of their time in technical skill: "The Damned Thing," "An Inhabitant of Carcosa," "The Eyes of the Panther," "Moxon's Master," and 20 more. 199pp. 5⅜ × 8½. 20767-6 Pa. $4.95

ETHICAL WRITINGS OF MAIMONIDES, Maimonides. Most significant ethical works of great medieval sage, newly translated for utmost precision, readability. Laws Concerning Character Traits, Eight Chapters, more. 192pp. 5⅜ × 8½.
24522-5 Pa. $4.50

THE EXPLORATION OF THE COLORADO RIVER AND ITS CANYONS, J. W. Powell. Full text of Powell's 1,000-mile expedition down the fabled Colorado in 1869. Superb account of terrain, geology, vegetation, Indians, famine, mutiny, treacherous rapids, mighty canyons, during exploration of last unknown part of continental U.S. 400pp. 5⅜ × 8½. 20094-9 Pa. $7.95

HISTORY OF PHILOSOPHY, Julián Marías. Clearest one-volume history on the market. Every major philosopher and dozens of others, to Existentialism and later. 505pp. 5⅜ × 8½. 21739-6 Pa. $9.95

ALL ABOUT LIGHTNING, Martin A. Uman. Highly readable non-technical survey of nature and causes of lightning, thunderstorms, ball lightning, St. Elmo's Fire, much more. Illustrated. 192pp. 5⅜ × 8½. 25237-X Pa. $5.95

SAILING ALONE AROUND THE WORLD, Captain Joshua Slocum. First man to sail around the world, alone, in small boat. One of great feats of seamanship told in delightful manner. 67 illustrations. 294pp. 5⅜ × 8½. 20326-3 Pa. $4.95

LETTERS AND NOTES ON THE MANNERS, CUSTOMS AND CONDITIONS OF THE NORTH AMERICAN INDIANS, George Catlin. Classic account of life among Plains Indians: ceremonies, hunt, warfare, etc. 312 plates. 572pp. of text. 6⅛ × 9¼. 22118-0, 22119-9, Pa. Two-vol. set $17.90

ALASKA: The Harriman Expedition, 1899, John Burroughs, John Muir, et al. Informative, engrossing accounts of two-month, 9,000-mile expedition. Native peoples, wildlife, forests, geography, salmon industry, glaciers, more. Profusely illustrated. 240 black-and-white line drawings. 124 black-and-white photographs. 3 maps. Index. 576pp. 5⅜ × 8½. 25109-8 Pa. $11.95

THE BOOK OF BEASTS: Being a Translation from a Latin Bestiary of the Twelfth Century, T. H. White. Wonderful catalog real and fanciful beasts: manticore, griffin, phoenix, amphivius, jaculus, many more. White's witty erudite commentary on scientific, historical aspects. Fascinating glimpse of medieval mind. Illustrated. 296pp. 5⅜ × 8¼. (Available in U.S. only)　24609-4 Pa. $6.95

FRANK LLOYD WRIGHT: ARCHITECTURE AND NATURE With 160 Illustrations, Donald Hoffmann. Profusely illustrated study of influence of nature—especially prairie—on Wright's designs for Fallingwater, Robie House, Guggenheim Museum, other masterpieces. 96pp. 9¼ × 10¾.　25098-9 Pa. $8.95

FRANK LLOYD WRIGHT'S FALLINGWATER, Donald Hoffmann. Wright's famous waterfall house: planning and construction of organic idea. History of site, owners, Wright's personal involvement. Photographs of various stages of building. Preface by Edgar Kaufmann, Jr. 100 illustrations. 112pp. 9¼ × 10.

23671-4 Pa. $8.95

YEARS WITH FRANK LLOYD WRIGHT: Apprentice to Genius, Edgar Tafel. Insightful memoir by a former apprentice presents a revealing portrait of Wright the man, the inspired teacher, the greatest American architect. 372 black-and-white illustrations. Preface. Index. vi + 228pp. 8¼ × 11.　24801-1 Pa. $10.95

THE STORY OF KING ARTHUR AND HIS KNIGHTS, Howard Pyle. Enchanting version of King Arthur fable has delighted generations with imaginative narratives of exciting adventures and unforgettable illustrations by the author. 41 illustrations. xviii + 313pp. 6⅛ × 9¼.　21445-1 Pa. $6.95

THE GODS OF THE EGYPTIANS, E. A. Wallis Budge. Thorough coverage of numerous gods of ancient Egypt by foremost Egyptologist. Information on evolution of cults, rites and gods; the cult of Osiris; the Book of the Dead and its rites; the sacred animals and birds; Heaven and Hell; and more. 956pp. 6⅛ × 9¼.

22055-9, 22056-7 Pa., Two-vol. set $21.90

A THEOLOGICO-POLITICAL TREATISE, Benedict Spinoza. Also contains unfinished *Political Treatise*. Great classic on religious liberty, theory of government on common consent. R. Elwes translation. Total of 421pp. 5⅜ × 8½.

20249-6 Pa. $7.95

INCIDENTS OF TRAVEL IN CENTRAL AMERICA, CHIAPAS, AND YUCATAN, John L. Stephens. Almost single-handed discovery of Maya culture; exploration of ruined cities, monuments, temples; customs of Indians. 115 drawings. 892pp. 5⅜ × 8½.　22404-X, 22405-8 Pa., Two-vol. set $15.90

LOS CAPRICHOS, Francisco Goya. 80 plates of wild, grotesque monsters and caricatures. Prado manuscript included. 183pp. 6⅜ × 9⅜.　22384-1 Pa. $5.95

AUTOBIOGRAPHY: The Story of My Experiments with Truth, Mohandas K. Gandhi. Not hagiography, but Gandhi in his own words. Boyhood, legal studies, purification, the growth of the Satyagraha (nonviolent protest) movement. Critical, inspiring work of the man who freed India. 480pp. 5⅜ × 8½. (Available in U.S. only)

24593-4 Pa. $6.95

ILLUSTRATED DICTIONARY OF HISTORIC ARCHITECTURE, edited by Cyril M. Harris. Extraordinary compendium of clear, concise definitions for over 5,000 important architectural terms complemented by over 2,000 line drawings. Covers full spectrum of architecture from ancient ruins to 20th-century Modernism. Preface. 592pp. 7½ × 9⅝. 24444-X Pa. $15.95

THE NIGHT BEFORE CHRISTMAS, Clement Moore. Full text, and woodcuts from original 1848 book. Also critical, historical material. 19 illustrations. 40pp. 4⅝ × 6. 22797-9 Pa. $2.50

THE LESSON OF JAPANESE ARCHITECTURE: 165 Photographs, Jiro Harada. Memorable gallery of 165 photographs taken in the 1930's of exquisite Japanese homes of the well-to-do and historic buildings. 13 line diagrams. 192pp. 8⅜ × 11¼. 24778-3 Pa. $10.95

THE AUTOBIOGRAPHY OF CHARLES DARWIN AND SELECTED LETTERS, edited by Francis Darwin. The fascinating life of eccentric genius composed of an intimate memoir by Darwin (intended for his children); commentary by his son, Francis; hundreds of fragments from notebooks, journals, papers; and letters to and from Lyell, Hooker, Huxley, Wallace and Henslow. xi + 365pp. 5⅜ × 8. 20479-0 Pa. $6.95

WONDERS OF THE SKY: Observing Rainbows, Comets, Eclipses, the Stars and Other Phenomena, Fred Schaaf. Charming, easy-to-read poetic guide to all manner of celestial events visible to the naked eye. Mock suns, glories, Belt of Venus, more. Illustrated. 299pp. 5¼ × 8¼. 24402-4 Pa. $7.95

BURNHAM'S CELESTIAL HANDBOOK, Robert Burnham, Jr. Thorough guide to the stars beyond our solar system. Exhaustive treatment. Alphabetical by constellation: Andromeda to Cetus in Vol. 1; Chamaeleon to Orion in Vol. 2; and Pavo to Vulpecula in Vol. 3. Hundreds of illustrations. Index in Vol. 3. 2,000pp. 6⅛ × 9¼. 23567-X, 23568-8, 23673-0 Pa., Three-vol. set $41.85

STAR NAMES: Their Lore and Meaning, Richard Hinckley Allen. Fascinating history of names various cultures have given to constellations and literary and folkloristic uses that have been made of stars. Indexes to subjects. Arabic and Greek names. Biblical references. Bibliography. 563pp. 5⅜ × 8½. 21079-0 Pa. $8.95

THIRTY YEARS THAT SHOOK PHYSICS: The Story of Quantum Theory, George Gamow. Lucid, accessible introduction to influential theory of energy and matter. Careful explanations of Dirac's anti-particles, Bohr's model of the atom, much more. 12 plates. Numerous drawings. 240pp. 5⅜ × 8½. 24895-X Pa. $5.95

CHINESE DOMESTIC FURNITURE IN PHOTOGRAPHS AND MEASURED DRAWINGS, Gustav Ecke. A rare volume, now affordably priced for antique collectors, furniture buffs and art historians. Detailed review of styles ranging from early Shang to late Ming. Unabridged republication. 161 black-and-white drawings, photos. Total of 224pp. 8⅜ × 11¼. (Available in U.S. only) 25171-3 Pa. $13.95

VINCENT VAN GOGH: A Biography, Julius Meier-Graefe. Dynamic, penetrating study of artist's life, relationship with brother, Theo, painting techniques, travels, more. Readable, engrossing. 160pp. 5⅜ × 8½. (Available in U.S. only) 25253-1 Pa. $4.95

HOW TO WRITE, Gertrude Stein. Gertrude Stein claimed anyone could understand her unconventional writing—here are clues to help. Fascinating improvisations, language experiments, explanations illuminate Stein's craft and the art of writing. Total of 414pp. 4⅝ × 6⅝. 23144-5 Pa. $6.95

ADVENTURES AT SEA IN THE GREAT AGE OF SAIL: Five Firsthand Narratives, edited by Elliot Snow. Rare true accounts of exploration, whaling, shipwreck, fierce natives, trade, shipboard life, more. 33 illustrations. Introduction. 353pp. 5⅜ × 8½. 25177-2 Pa. $8.95

THE HERBAL OR GENERAL HISTORY OF PLANTS, John Gerard. Classic descriptions of about 2,850 plants—with over 2,700 illustrations—includes Latin and English names, physical descriptions, varieties, time and place of growth, more. 2,706 illustrations. xlv + 1,678pp. 8½ × 12¼. 23147-X Cloth. $75.00

DOROTHY AND THE WIZARD IN OZ, L. Frank Baum. Dorothy and the Wizard visit the center of the Earth, where people are vegetables, glass houses grow and Oz characters reappear. Classic sequel to *Wizard of Oz*. 256pp. 5⅜ × 8.
24714-7 Pa. $5.95

SONGS OF EXPERIENCE: Facsimile Reproduction with 26 Plates in Full Color, William Blake. This facsimile of Blake's original "Illuminated Book" reproduces 26 full-color plates from a rare 1826 edition. Includes "The Tyger," "London," "Holy Thursday," and other immortal poems. 26 color plates. Printed text of poems. 48pp. 5¼ × 7. 24636-1 Pa. $3.95

SONGS OF INNOCENCE, William Blake. The first and most popular of Blake's famous "Illuminated Books," in a facsimile edition reproducing all 31 brightly colored plates. Additional printed text of each poem. 64pp. 5¼ × 7.
22764-2 Pa. $3.95

PRECIOUS STONES, Max Bauer. Classic, thorough study of diamonds, rubies, emeralds, garnets, etc.: physical character, occurrence, properties, use, similar topics. 20 plates, 8 in color. 94 figures. 659pp. 6⅛ × 9¼.
21910-0, 21911-9 Pa., Two-vol. set $15.90

ENCYCLOPEDIA OF VICTORIAN NEEDLEWORK, S. F. A. Caulfeild and Blanche Saward. Full, precise descriptions of stitches, techniques for dozens of needlecrafts—most exhaustive reference of its kind. Over 800 figures. Total of 679pp. 8⅛ × 11. Two volumes. Vol. 1 22800-2 Pa. $11.95
Vol. 2 22801-0 Pa. $11.95

THE MARVELOUS LAND OF OZ, L. Frank Baum. Second Oz book, the Scarecrow and Tin Woodman are back with hero named Tip, Oz magic. 136 illustrations. 287pp. 5⅜ × 8½. 20692-0 Pa. $5.95

WILD FOWL DECOYS, Joel Barber. Basic book on the subject, by foremost authority and collector. Reveals history of decoy making and rigging, place in American culture, different kinds of decoys, how to make them, and how to use them. 140 plates. 156pp. 7⅞ × 10¾. 20011-6 Pa. $8.95

HISTORY OF LACE, Mrs. Bury Palliser. Definitive, profusely illustrated chronicle of lace from earliest times to late 19th century. Laces of Italy, Greece, England, France, Belgium, etc. Landmark of needlework scholarship. 266 illustrations. 672pp. 6⅛ × 9¼. 24742-2 Pa. $14.95

ILLUSTRATED GUIDE TO SHAKER FURNITURE, Robert Meader. All furniture and appurtenances, with much on unknown local styles. 235 photos. 146pp. 9 × 12. 22819-3 Pa. $8.95

WHALE SHIPS AND WHALING: A Pictorial Survey, George Francis Dow. Over 200 vintage engravings, drawings, photographs of barks, brigs, cutters, other vessels. Also harpoons, lances, whaling guns, many other artifacts. Comprehensive text by foremost authority. 207 black-and-white illustrations. 288pp. 6 × 9.
24808-9 Pa. $9.95

THE BERTRAMS, Anthony Trollope. Powerful portrayal of blind self-will and thwarted ambition includes one of Trollope's most heartrending love stories. 497pp. 5⅜ × 8½. 25119-5 Pa. $9.95

ADVENTURES WITH A HAND LENS, Richard Headstrom. Clearly written guide to observing and studying flowers and grasses, fish scales, moth and insect wings, egg cases, buds, feathers, seeds, leaf scars, moss, molds, ferns, common crystals, etc.—all with an ordinary, inexpensive magnifying glass. 209 exact line drawings aid in your discoveries. 220pp. 5⅜ × 8½. 23330-8 Pa. $4.95

RODIN ON ART AND ARTISTS, Auguste Rodin. Great sculptor's candid, wide-ranging comments on meaning of art; great artists; relation of sculpture to poetry, painting, music; philosophy of life, more. 76 superb black-and-white illustrations of Rodin's sculpture, drawings and prints. 119pp. 8⅜ × 11¼. 24487-3 Pa. $7.95

FIFTY CLASSIC FRENCH FILMS, 1912–1982: A Pictorial Record, Anthony Slide. Memorable stills from Grand Illusion, Beauty and the Beast, Hiroshima, Mon Amour, many more. Credits, plot synopses, reviews, etc. 160pp. 8¼ × 11.
25256-6 Pa. $11.95

THE PRINCIPLES OF PSYCHOLOGY, William James. Famous long course complete, unabridged. Stream of thought, time perception, memory, experimental methods; great work decades ahead of its time. 94 figures. 1,391pp. 5⅜ × 8½.
20381-6, 20382-4 Pa., Two-vol. set $23.90

BODIES IN A BOOKSHOP, R. T. Campbell. Challenging mystery of blackmail and murder with ingenious plot and superbly drawn characters. In the best tradition of British suspense fiction. 192pp. 5⅜ × 8½. 24720-1 Pa. $4.95

CALLAS: PORTRAIT OF A PRIMA DONNA, George Jellinek. Renowned commentator on the musical scene chronicles incredible career and life of the most controversial, fascinating, influential operatic personality of our time. 64 black-and-white photographs. 416pp. 5⅜ × 8¼. 25047-4 Pa. $8.95

GEOMETRY, RELATIVITY AND THE FOURTH DIMENSION, Rudolph Rucker. Exposition of fourth dimension, concepts of relativity as Flatland characters continue adventures. Popular, easily followed yet accurate, profound. 141 illustrations. 133pp. 5⅜ × 8½. 23400-2 Pa. $4.95

HOUSEHOLD STORIES BY THE BROTHERS GRIMM, with pictures by Walter Crane. 53 classic stories—Rumpelstiltskin, Rapunzel, Hansel and Gretel, the Fisherman and his Wife, Snow White, Tom Thumb, Sleeping Beauty, Cinderella, and so much more—lavishly illustrated with original 19th century drawings. 114 illustrations. x + 269pp. 5⅜ × 8½. 21080-4 Pa. $4.95

SUNDIALS, Albert Waugh. Far and away the best, most thorough coverage of ideas, mathematics concerned, types, construction, adjusting anywhere. Over 100 illustrations. 230pp. 5⅜ × 8½. 22947-5 Pa. $5.95

PICTURE HISTORY OF THE NORMANDIE: With 190 Illustrations, Frank O. Braynard. Full story of legendary French ocean liner: Art Deco interiors, design innovations, furnishings, celebrities, maiden voyage, tragic fire, much more. Extensive text. 144pp. 8⅜ × 11¾. 25257-4 Pa. $10.95

THE FIRST AMERICAN COOKBOOK: A Facsimile of "American Cookery," 1796, Amelia Simmons. Facsimile of the first American-written cookbook published in the United States contains authentic recipes for colonial favorites—pumpkin pudding, winter squash pudding, spruce beer, Indian slapjacks, and more. Introductory Essay and Glossary of colonial cooking terms. 80pp. 5⅜ × 8½. 24710-4 Pa. $3.50

101 PUZZLES IN THOUGHT AND LOGIC, C. R. Wylie, Jr. Solve murders and robberies, find out which fishermen are liars, how a blind man could possibly identify a color—purely by your own reasoning! 107pp. 5⅜ × 8½. 20367-0 Pa. $2.50

ANCIENT EGYPTIAN MYTHS AND LEGENDS, Lewis Spence. Examines animism, totemism, fetishism, creation myths, deities, alchemy, art and magic, other topics. Over 50 illustrations. 432pp. 5⅜ × 8½. 26525-0 Pa. $8.95

ANTHROPOLOGY AND MODERN LIFE, Franz Boas. Great anthropologist's classic treatise on race and culture. Introduction by Ruth Bunzel. Only inexpensive paperback edition. 255pp. 5⅜ × 8½. 25245-0 Pa. $6.95

THE TALE OF PETER RABBIT, Beatrix Potter. The inimitable Peter's terrifying adventure in Mr. McGregor's garden, with all 27 wonderful, full-color Potter illustrations. 55pp. 4¼ × 5½. (Available in U.S. only) 22827-4 Pa. $1.75

THREE PROPHETIC SCIENCE FICTION NOVELS, H. G. Wells. *When the Sleeper Wakes, A Story of the Days to Come* and *The Time Machine* (full version). 335pp. 5⅜ × 8½. (Available in U.S. only) 20605-X Pa. $6.95

APICIUS COOKERY AND DINING IN IMPERIAL ROME, edited and translated by Joseph Dommers Vehling. Oldest known cookbook in existence offers readers a clear picture of what foods Romans ate, how they prepared them, etc. 49 illustrations. 301pp. 6⅛ × 9¼. 23563-7 Pa. $7.95

SHAKESPEARE LEXICON AND QUOTATION DICTIONARY, Alexander Schmidt. Full definitions, locations, shades of meaning of every word in plays and poems. More than 50,000 exact quotations. 1,485pp. 6½ × 9¼. 22726-X, 22727-8 Pa., Two-vol. set $31.90

THE WORLD'S GREAT SPEECHES, edited by Lewis Copeland and Lawrence W. Lamm. Vast collection of 278 speeches from Greeks to 1970. Powerful and effective models; unique look at history. 842pp. 5⅜ × 8½. 20468-5 Pa. $12.95

THE BLUE FAIRY BOOK, Andrew Lang. The first, most famous collection, with many familiar tales: Little Red Riding Hood, Aladdin and the Wonderful Lamp, Puss in Boots, Sleeping Beauty, Hansel and Gretel, Rumpelstiltskin; 37 in all. 138 illustrations. 390pp. 5⅜ × 8½. 21437-0 Pa. $6.95

THE STORY OF THE CHAMPIONS OF THE ROUND TABLE, Howard Pyle. Sir Launcelot, Sir Tristram and Sir Percival in spirited adventures of love and triumph retold in Pyle's inimitable style. 50 drawings, 31 full-page. xviii + 329pp. 6½ × 9¼. 21883-X Pa. $7.95

THE MYTHS OF THE NORTH AMERICAN INDIANS, Lewis Spence. Myths and legends of the Algonquins, Iroquois, Pawnees and Sioux with comprehensive historical and ethnological commentary. 36 illustrations. 5⅜ × 8½.
25967-6 Pa. $8.95

GREAT DINOSAUR HUNTERS AND THEIR DISCOVERIES, Edwin H. Colbert. Fascinating, lavishly illustrated chronicle of dinosaur research, 1820's to 1960. Achievements of Cope, Marsh, Brown, Buckland, Mantell, Huxley, many others. 384pp. 5¼ × 8¼. 24701-5 Pa. $7.95

THE TASTEMAKERS, Russell Lynes. Informal, illustrated social history of American taste 1850's–1950's. First popularized categories Highbrow, Lowbrow, Middlebrow. 129 illustrations. New (1979) afterword. 384pp. 6 × 9.
23993-4 Pa. $8.95

DOUBLE CROSS PURPOSES, Ronald A. Knox. A treasure hunt in the Scottish Highlands, an old map, unidentified corpse, surprise discoveries keep reader guessing in this cleverly intricate tale of financial skullduggery. 2 black-and-white maps. 320pp. 5⅜ × 8½. (Available in U.S. only) 25032-6 Pa. $6.95

AUTHENTIC VICTORIAN DECORATION AND ORNAMENTATION IN FULL COLOR: 46 Plates from "Studies in Design," Christopher Dresser. Superb full-color lithographs reproduced from rare original portfolio of a major Victorian designer. 48pp. 9¼ × 12¼. 25083-0 Pa. $7.95

PRIMITIVE ART, Franz Boas. Remains the best text ever prepared on subject, thoroughly discussing Indian, African, Asian, Australian, and, especially, Northern American primitive art. Over 950 illustrations show ceramics, masks, totem poles, weapons, textiles, paintings, much more. 376pp. 5⅜ × 8. 20025-6 Pa. $7.95

SIDELIGHTS ON RELATIVITY, Albert Einstein. Unabridged republication of two lectures delivered by the great physicist in 1920–21. *Ether and Relativity* and *Geometry and Experience*. Elegant ideas in non-mathematical form, accessible to intelligent layman. vi + 56pp. 5⅜ × 8½. 24511-X Pa. $2.95

THE WIT AND HUMOR OF OSCAR WILDE, edited by Alvin Redman. More than 1,000 ripostes, paradoxes, wisecracks: Work is the curse of the drinking classes, I can resist everything except temptation, etc. 258pp. 5⅜ × 8½. 20602-5 Pa. $4.95

ADVENTURES WITH A MICROSCOPE, Richard Headstrom. 59 adventures with clothing fibers, protozoa, ferns and lichens, roots and leaves, much more. 142 illustrations. 232pp. 5⅜ × 8½. 23471-1 Pa. $3.95

PLANTS OF THE BIBLE, Harold N. Moldenke and Alma L. Moldenke. Standard reference to all 230 plants mentioned in Scriptures. Latin name, biblical reference, uses, modern identity, much more. Unsurpassed encyclopedic resource for scholars, botanists, nature lovers, students of Bible. Bibliography. Indexes. 123 black-and-white illustrations. 384pp. 6 × 9. 25069-5 Pa. $8.95

FAMOUS AMERICAN WOMEN: A Biographical Dictionary from Colonial Times to the Present, Robert McHenry, ed. From Pocahontas to Rosa Parks, 1,035 distinguished American women documented in separate biographical entries. Accurate, up-to-date data, numerous categories, spans 400 years. Indices. 493pp. 6½ × 9¼. 24523-3 Pa. $10.95

THE FABULOUS INTERIORS OF THE GREAT OCEAN LINERS IN HISTORIC PHOTOGRAPHS, William H. Miller, Jr. Some 200 superb photographs capture exquisite interiors of world's great "floating palaces"—1890's to 1980's: *Titanic, Ile de France, Queen Elizabeth, United States, Europa,* more. Approx. 200 black-and-white photographs. Captions. Text. Introduction. 160pp. 8⅞ × 11¾. 24756-2 Pa. $9.95

THE GREAT LUXURY LINERS, 1927–1954: A Photographic Record, William H. Miller, Jr. Nostalgic tribute to heyday of ocean liners. 186 photos of Ile de France, Normandie, Leviathan, Queen Elizabeth, United States, many others. Interior and exterior views. Introduction. Captions. 160pp. 9 × 12. 24056-8 Pa. $10.95

A NATURAL HISTORY OF THE DUCKS, John Charles Phillips. Great landmark of ornithology offers complete detailed coverage of nearly 200 species and subspecies of ducks: gadwall, sheldrake, merganser, pintail, many more. 74 full-color plates, 102 black-and-white. Bibliography. Total of 1,920pp. 8⅝ × 11¼. 25141-1, 25142-X Cloth. Two-vol. set $100.00

THE SEAWEED HANDBOOK: An Illustrated Guide to Seaweeds from North Carolina to Canada, Thomas F. Lee. Concise reference covers 78 species. Scientific and common names, habitat, distribution, more. Finding keys for easy identification. 224pp. 5⅜ × 8½. 25215-9 Pa. $6.95

THE TEN BOOKS OF ARCHITECTURE: The 1755 Leoni Edition, Leon Battista Alberti. Rare classic helped introduce the glories of ancient architecture to the Renaissance. 68 black-and-white plates. 336pp. 8⅜ × 11¼. 25239-6 Pa. $14.95

MISS MACKENZIE, Anthony Trollope. Minor masterpieces by Victorian master unmasks many truths about life in 19th-century England. First inexpensive edition in years. 392pp. 5⅜ × 8½. 25201-9 Pa. $8.95

THE RIME OF THE ANCIENT MARINER, Gustave Doré, Samuel Taylor Coleridge. Dramatic engravings considered by many to be his greatest work. The terrifying space of the open sea, the storms and whirlpools of an unknown ocean, the ice of Antarctica, more—all rendered in a powerful, chilling manner. Full text. 38 plates. 77pp. 9¼ × 12. 22305-1 Pa. $4.95

THE EXPEDITIONS OF ZEBULON MONTGOMERY PIKE, Zebulon Montgomery Pike. Fascinating first-hand accounts (1805–6) of exploration of Mississippi River, Indian wars, capture by Spanish dragoons, much more. 1,088pp. 5⅜ × 8½. 25254-X, 25255-8 Pa. Two-vol. set $25.90

A CONCISE HISTORY OF PHOTOGRAPHY: Third Revised Edition, Helmut Gernsheim. Best one-volume history—camera obscura, photochemistry, daguerreotypes, evolution of cameras, film, more. Also artistic aspects—landscape, portraits, fine art, etc. 281 black-and-white photographs. 26 in color. 176pp. 8⅜ × 11¼. 25128-4 Pa. $13.95

THE DORÉ BIBLE ILLUSTRATIONS, Gustave Doré. 241 detailed plates from the Bible: the Creation scenes, Adam and Eve, Flood, Babylon, battle sequences, life of Jesus, etc. Each plate is accompanied by the verses from the King James version of the Bible. 241pp. 9 × 12. 23004-X Pa. $9.95

WANDERINGS IN WEST AFRICA, Richard F. Burton. Great Victorian scholar/adventurer's invaluable descriptions of African tribal rituals, fetishism, culture, art, much more. Fascinating 19th-century account. 624pp. 5⅜ × 8½. 26890-X Pa. $12.95

FLATLAND, E. A. Abbott. Intriguing and enormously popular science-fiction classic explores the complexities of trying to survive as a two-dimensional being in a three-dimensional world. Amusingly illustrated by the author. 16 illustrations. 103pp. 5⅜ × 8½. 20001-9 Pa. $2.50

THE HISTORY OF THE LEWIS AND CLARK EXPEDITION, Meriwether Lewis and William Clark, edited by Elliott Coues. Classic edition of Lewis and Clark's day-by-day journals that later became the basis for U.S. claims to Oregon and the West. Accurate and invaluable geographical, botanical, biological, meteorological and anthropological material. Total of 1,508pp. 5⅜ × 8½.
21268-8, 21269-6, 21270-X Pa. Three-vol. set $26.85

LANGUAGE, TRUTH AND LOGIC, Alfred J. Ayer. Famous, clear introduction to Vienna, Cambridge schools of Logical Positivism. Role of philosophy, elimination of metaphysics, nature of analysis, etc. 160pp. 5⅜ × 8½. (Available in U.S. and Canada only) 20010-8 Pa. $3.95

MATHEMATICS FOR THE NONMATHEMATICIAN, Morris Kline. Detailed, college-level treatment of mathematics in cultural and historical context, with numerous exercises. For liberal arts students. Preface. Recommended Reading Lists. Tables. Index. Numerous black-and-white figures. xvi + 641pp. 5⅜ × 8½.
24823-2 Pa. $11.95

HANDBOOK OF PICTORIAL SYMBOLS, Rudolph Modley. 3,250 signs and symbols, many systems in full; official or heavy commercial use. Arranged by subject. Most in Pictorial Archive series. 143pp. 8⅛ × 11. 23357-X Pa. $6.95

INCIDENTS OF TRAVEL IN YUCATAN, John L. Stephens. Classic (1843) exploration of jungles of Yucatan, looking for evidences of Maya civilization. Travel adventures, Mexican and Indian culture, etc. Total of 669pp. 5⅜ × 8½.
20926-1, 20927-X Pa., Two-vol. set $11.90

DEGAS: An Intimate Portrait, Ambroise Vollard. Charming, anecdotal memoir by famous art dealer of one of the greatest 19th-century French painters. 14 black-and-white illustrations. Introduction by Harold L. Van Doren. 96pp. 5⅜ × 8½.
25131-4 Pa. $4.95

PERSONAL NARRATIVE OF A PILGRIMAGE TO ALMANDINAH AND MECCAH, Richard Burton. Great travel classic by remarkably colorful personality. Burton, disguised as a Moroccan, visited sacred shrines of Islam, narrowly escaping death. 47 illustrations. 959pp. 5⅜ × 8½.    21217-3, 21218-1 Pa., Two-vol. set $19.90

PHRASE AND WORD ORIGINS, A. H. Holt. Entertaining, reliable, modern study of more than 1,200 colorful words, phrases, origins and histories. Much unexpected information. 254pp. 5⅜ × 8½.    20758-7 Pa. $5.95

THE RED THUMB MARK, R. Austin Freeman. In this first Dr. Thorndyke case, the great scientific detective draws fascinating conclusions from the nature of a single fingerprint. Exciting story, authentic science. 320pp. 5⅜ × 8½. (Available in U.S. only)    25210-8 Pa. $6.95

AN EGYPTIAN HIEROGLYPHIC DICTIONARY, E. A. Wallis Budge. Monumental work containing about 25,000 words or terms that occur in texts ranging from 3000 B.C. to 600 A.D. Each entry consists of a transliteration of the word, the word in hieroglyphs, and the meaning in English. 1,314pp. 6⅜ × 10.
23615-3, 23616-1 Pa., Two-vol. set $35.90

THE COMPLEAT STRATEGYST: Being a Primer on the Theory of Games of Strategy, J. D. Williams. Highly entertaining classic describes, with many illustrated examples, how to select best strategies in conflict situations. Prefaces. Appendices. xvi + 268pp. 5⅜ × 8½.    25101-2 Pa. $6.95

THE ROAD TO OZ, L. Frank Baum. Dorothy meets the Shaggy Man, little Button-Bright and the Rainbow's beautiful daughter in this delightful trip to the magical Land of Oz. 272pp. 5⅜ × 8.    25208-6 Pa. $5.95

POINT AND LINE TO PLANE, Wassily Kandinsky. Seminal exposition of role of point, line, other elements in non-objective painting. Essential to understanding 20th-century art. 127 illustrations. 192pp. 6½ × 9¼.    23808-3 Pa. $5.95

LADY ANNA, Anthony Trollope. Moving chronicle of Countess Lovel's bitter struggle to win for herself and daughter Anna their rightful rank and fortune—perhaps at cost of sanity itself. 384pp. 5⅜ × 8½.    24669-8 Pa. $8.95

EGYPTIAN MAGIC, E. A. Wallis Budge. Sums up all that is known about magic in Ancient Egypt: the role of magic in controlling the gods, powerful amulets that warded off evil spirits, scarabs of immortality, use of wax images, formulas and spells, the secret name, much more. 253pp. 5⅜ × 8½.    22681-6 Pa. $4.50

THE DANCE OF SIVA, Ananda Coomaraswamy. Preeminent authority unfolds the vast metaphysic of India: the revelation of her art, conception of the universe, social organization, etc. 27 reproductions of art masterpieces. 192pp. 5⅜ × 8½.
24817-8 Pa. $5.95

CHRISTMAS CUSTOMS AND TRADITIONS, Clement A. Miles. Origin, evolution, significance of religious, secular practices. Caroling, gifts, yule logs, much more. Full, scholarly yet fascinating; non-sectarian. 400pp. 5⅜ × 8½.
23354-5 Pa. $6.95

THE HUMAN FIGURE IN MOTION, Eadweard Muybridge. More than 4,500 stopped-action photos, in action series, showing undraped men, women, children jumping, lying down, throwing, sitting, wrestling, carrying, etc. 390pp. 7⅞ × 10⅝.
20204-6 Cloth. $24.95

THE MAN WHO WAS THURSDAY, Gilbert Keith Chesterton. Witty, fast-paced novel about a club of anarchists in turn-of-the-century London. Brilliant social, religious, philosophical speculations. 128pp. 5⅜ × 8½.
25121-7 Pa. $3.95

A CEZANNE SKETCHBOOK: Figures, Portraits, Landscapes and Still Lifes, Paul Cezanne. Great artist experiments with tonal effects, light, mass, other qualities in over 100 drawings. A revealing view of developing master painter, precursor of Cubism. 102 black-and-white illustrations. 144pp. 8¾ × 6⅝.
24790-2 Pa. $6.95

AN ENCYCLOPEDIA OF BATTLES: Accounts of Over 1,560 Battles from 1479 B.C. to the Present, David Eggenberger. Presents essential details of every major battle in recorded history, from the first battle of Megiddo in 1479 B.C. to Grenada in 1984. List of Battle Maps. New Appendix covering the years 1967–1984. Index. 99 illustrations. 544pp. 6½ × 9¼.
24913-1 Pa. $14.95

AN ETYMOLOGICAL DICTIONARY OF MODERN ENGLISH, Ernest Weekley. Richest, fullest work, by foremost British lexicographer. Detailed word histories. Inexhaustible. Total of 856pp. 6½ × 9¼.
21873-2, 21874-0 Pa., Two-vol. set $19.90

WEBSTER'S AMERICAN MILITARY BIOGRAPHIES, edited by Robert McHenry. Over 1,000 figures who shaped 3 centuries of American military history. Detailed biographies of Nathan Hale, Douglas MacArthur, Mary Hallaren, others. Chronologies of engagements, more. Introduction. Addenda. 1,033 entries in alphabetical order. xi + 548pp. 6½ × 9¼. (Available in U.S. only)
24758-9 Pa. $13.95

LIFE IN ANCIENT EGYPT, Adolf Erman. Detailed older account, with much not in more recent books: domestic life, religion, magic, medicine, commerce, and whatever else needed for complete picture. Many illustrations. 597pp. 5⅜ × 8½.
22632-8 Pa. $8.95

HISTORIC COSTUME IN PICTURES, Braun & Schneider. Over 1,450 costumed figures shown, covering a wide variety of peoples: kings, emperors, nobles, priests, servants, soldiers, scholars, townsfolk, peasants, merchants, courtiers, cavaliers, and more. 256pp. 8⅜ × 11¼.
23150-X Pa. $9.95

THE NOTEBOOKS OF LEONARDO DA VINCI, edited by J. P. Richter. Extracts from manuscripts reveal great genius; on painting, sculpture, anatomy, sciences, geography, etc. Both Italian and English. 186 ms. pages reproduced, plus 500 additional drawings, including studies for *Last Supper, Sforza* monument, etc. 860pp. 7⅞ × 10¾. (Available in U.S. only) 22572-0, 22573-9 Pa., Two-vol. set $31.90

THE ART NOUVEAU STYLE BOOK OF ALPHONSE MUCHA: All 72 Plates from "Documents Decoratifs" in Original Color, Alphonse Mucha. Rare copyright-free design portfolio by high priest of Art Nouveau. Jewelry, wallpaper, stained glass, furniture, figure studies, plant and animal motifs, etc. Only complete one-volume edition. 80pp. 9⅜ × 12¼. 24044-4 Pa. $9.95

ANIMALS: 1,419 COPYRIGHT-FREE ILLUSTRATIONS OF MAMMALS, BIRDS, FISH, INSECTS, ETC., edited by Jim Harter. Clear wood engravings present, in extremely lifelike poses, over 1,000 species of animals. One of the most extensive pictorial sourcebooks of its kind. Captions. Index. 284pp. 9 × 12.
23766-4 Pa. $9.95

OBELISTS FLY HIGH, C. Daly King. Masterpiece of American detective fiction, long out of print, involves murder on a 1935 transcontinental flight—"a very thrilling story"—NY Times. Unabridged and unaltered republication of the edition published by William Collins Sons & Co. Ltd., London, 1935. 288pp. 5⅜ × 8½. (Available in U.S. only) 25036-9 Pa. $5.95

VICTORIAN AND EDWARDIAN FASHION: A Photographic Survey, Alison Gernsheim. First fashion history completely illustrated by contemporary photographs. Full text plus 235 photos, 1840–1914, in which many celebrities appear. 240pp. 6½ × 9¼. 24205-6 Pa. $8.95

THE ART OF THE FRENCH ILLUSTRATED BOOK, 1700–1914, Gordon N. Ray. Over 630 superb book illustrations by Fragonard, Delacroix, Daumier, Doré, Grandville, Manet, Mucha, Steinlen, Toulouse-Lautrec and many others. Preface. Introduction. 633 halftones. Indices of artists, authors & titles, binders and provenances. Appendices. Bibliography. 608pp. 8⅜ × 11¼. 25086-5 Pa. $24.95

THE WONDERFUL WIZARD OF OZ, L. Frank Baum. Facsimile in full color of America's finest children's classic. 143 illustrations by W. W. Denslow. 267pp. 5⅜ × 8½. 20691-2 Pa. $7.95

FOLLOWING THE EQUATOR: A Journey Around the World, Mark Twain. Great writer's 1897 account of circumnavigating the globe by steamship. Ironic humor, keen observations, vivid and fascinating descriptions of exotic places. 197 illustrations. 720pp. 5⅜ × 8½. 26113-1 Pa. $15.95

THE FRIENDLY STARS, Martha Evans Martin & Donald Howard Menzel. Classic text marshalls the stars together in an engaging, non-technical survey, presenting them as sources of beauty in night sky. 23 illustrations. Foreword. 2 star charts. Index. 147pp. 5⅜ × 8½. 21099-5 Pa. $3.95

FADS AND FALLACIES IN THE NAME OF SCIENCE, Martin Gardner. Fair, witty appraisal of cranks, quacks, and quackeries of science and pseudoscience: hollow earth, Velikovsky, orgone energy, Dianetics, flying saucers, Bridey Murphy, food and medical fads, etc. Revised, expanded In the Name of Science. "A very able and even-tempered presentation."—The New Yorker. 363pp. 5⅜ × 8.
20394-8 Pa. $6.95

ANCIENT EGYPT: ITS CULTURE AND HISTORY, J. E Manchip White. From pre-dynastics through Ptolemies: society, history, political structure, religion, daily life, literature, cultural heritage. 48 plates. 217pp. 5⅜ × 8½. 22548-8 Pa. $5.95

# CATALOG OF DOVER BOOKS

SIR HARRY HOTSPUR OF HUMBLETHWAITE, Anthony Trollope. Incisive, unconventional psychological study of a conflict between a wealthy baronet, his idealistic daughter, and their scapegrace cousin. The 1870 novel in its first inexpensive edition in years. 250pp. 5⅜ × 8½. 24953-0 Pa. $6.95

LASERS AND HOLOGRAPHY, Winston E. Kock. Sound introduction to burgeoning field, expanded (1981) for second edition. Wave patterns, coherence, lasers, diffraction, zone plates, properties of holograms, recent advances. 84 illustrations. 160pp. 5⅜ × 8¼. (Except in United Kingdom) 24041-X Pa. $3.95

INTRODUCTION TO ARTIFICIAL INTELLIGENCE: SECOND, EN-LARGED EDITION, Philip C. Jackson, Jr. Comprehensive survey of artificial intelligence—the study of how machines (computers) can be made to act intelligently. Includes introductory and advanced material. Extensive notes updating the main text. 132 black-and-white illustrations. 512pp. 5⅜ × 8½. 24864-X Pa. $8.95

HISTORY OF INDIAN AND INDONESIAN ART, Ananda K. Coomaraswamy. Over 400 illustrations illuminate classic study of Indian art from earliest Harappa finds to early 20th century. Provides philosophical, religious and social insights. 304pp. 6⅛ × 9⅜. 25005-9 Pa. $11.95

THE GOLEM, Gustav Meyrink. Most famous supernatural novel in modern European literature, set in Ghetto of Old Prague around 1890. Compelling story of mystical experiences, strange transformations, profound terror. 13 black-and-white illustrations. 224pp. 5⅜ × 8½. (Available in U.S. only) 25025-3 Pa. $6.95

PICTORIAL ENCYCLOPEDIA OF HISTORIC ARCHITECTURAL PLANS, DETAILS AND ELEMENTS: With 1,880 Line Drawings of Arches, Domes, Doorways, Facades, Gables, Windows, etc., John Theodore Haneman. Sourcebook of inspiration for architects, designers, others. Bibliography. Captions. 141pp. 9 × 12. 24605-1 Pa. $7.95

BENCHLEY LOST AND FOUND, Robert Benchley. Finest humor from early 30's, about pet peeves, child psychologists, post office and others. Mostly unavailable elsewhere. 73 illustrations by Peter Arno and others. 183pp. 5⅜ × 8½. 22410-4 Pa. $4.95

ERTÉ GRAPHICS, Erté. Collection of striking color graphics: *Seasons, Alphabet, Numerals, Aces* and *Precious Stones.* 50 plates, including 4 on covers. 48pp. 9⅜ × 12¼. 23580-7 Pa. $7.95

THE JOURNAL OF HENRY D. THOREAU, edited by Bradford Torrey, F. H. Allen. Complete reprinting of 14 volumes, 1837–61, over two million words; the sourcebooks for *Walden*, etc. Definitive. All original sketches, plus 75 photographs. 1,804pp. 8½ × 12¼. 20312-3, 20313-1 Cloth., Two-vol. set $125.00

CASTLES: THEIR CONSTRUCTION AND HISTORY, Sidney Toy. Traces castle development from ancient roots. Nearly 200 photographs and drawings illustrate moats, keeps, baileys, many other features. Caernarvon, Dover Castles, Hadrian's Wall, Tower of London, dozens more. 256pp. 5⅜ × 8¼. 24898-4 Pa. $6.95

AMERICAN CLIPPER SHIPS: 1833–1858, Octavius T. Howe & Frederick C. Matthews. Fully-illustrated, encyclopedic review of 352 clipper ships from the period of America's greatest maritime supremacy. Introduction. 109 halftones. 5 black-and-white line illustrations. Index. Total of 928pp. 5⅜ × 8½.
25115-2, 25116-0 Pa., Two-vol. set $17.90

TOWARDS A NEW ARCHITECTURE, Le Corbusier. Pioneering manifesto by great architect, near legendary founder of "International School." Technical and aesthetic theories, views on industry, economics, relation of form to function, "mass-production spirit," much more. Profusely illustrated. Unabridged translation of 13th French edition. Introduction by Frederick Etchells. 320pp. 6⅛ × 9¼. (Available in U.S. only) 25023-7 Pa. $8.95

THE BOOK OF KELLS, edited by Blanche Cirker. Inexpensive collection of 32 full-color, full-page plates from the greatest illuminated manuscript of the Middle Ages, painstakingly reproduced from rare facsimile edition. Publisher's Note. Captions. 32pp. 9⅜ × 12¼. 24345-1 Pa. $4.95

BEST SCIENCE FICTION STORIES OF H. G. WELLS, H. G. Wells. Full novel *The Invisible Man*, plus 17 short stories: "The Crystal Egg," "Aepyornis Island," "The Strange Orchid," etc. 303pp. 5⅜ × 8½. (Available in U.S. only)
21531-8 Pa. $6.95

AMERICAN SAILING SHIPS: Their Plans and History, Charles G. Davis. Photos, construction details of schooners, frigates, clippers, other sailcraft of 18th to early 20th centuries—plus entertaining discourse on design, rigging, nautical lore, much more. 137 black-and-white illustrations. 240pp. 6⅛ × 9¼.
24658-2 Pa. $6.95

ENTERTAINING MATHEMATICAL PUZZLES, Martin Gardner. Selection of author's favorite conundrums involving arithmetic, money, speed, etc., with lively commentary. Complete solutions. 112pp. 5⅜ × 8½. 25211-6 Pa. $2.95

THE WILL TO BELIEVE, HUMAN IMMORTALITY, William James. Two books bound together. Effect of irrational on logical, and arguments for human immortality. 402pp. 5⅜ × 8½. 20291-7 Pa. $7.95

THE HAUNTED MONASTERY and THE CHINESE MAZE MURDERS, Robert Van Gulik. 2 full novels by Van Gulik continue adventures of Judge Dee and his companions. An evil Taoist monastery, seemingly supernatural events; overgrown topiary maze that hides strange crimes. Set in 7th-century China. 27 illustrations. 328pp. 5⅜ × 8½. 23502-5 Pa. $6.95

CELEBRATED CASES OF JUDGE DEE (DEE GOONG AN), translated by Robert Van Gulik. Authentic 18th-century Chinese detective novel; Dee and associates solve three interlocked cases. Led to Van Gulik's own stories with same characters. Extensive introduction. 9 illustrations. 237pp. 5⅜ × 8½.
23337-5 Pa. $5.95

*Prices subject to change without notice.*
Available at your book dealer or write for free catalog to Dept. GI, Dover Publications, Inc., 31 East 2nd St., Mineola, N.Y. 11501. Dover publishes more than 175 books each year on science, elementary and advanced mathematics, biology, music, art, literary history, social sciences and other areas.